SAS® Macro Language
Course Notes

Gwyn Saylor

OPTIONS
SYMBOLGEN
MPRINT
MLOGIC

SAS Institute Inc.
SAS Campus Drive
Cary, NC 27513

SAS® Macro Language Course Notes was written by **Jeff Cartier**. Course development coordination was provided by **Amy Peters**. Course development support was provided by **Michi Inagaki** and **Randy Stoltz**. Reviews of the Notes were provided by **Pat Herbert, Fritz Lehman, Marje Martin, Donna Martinez, Susan O'Connor, Bill Powers** and **J. Larry Stewart**. Production coordination was provided by **Kandis Moore** with assistance from **Inetta Hinton, Kandy Newton**, and **Gloria Walker**.

SAS INSTITUTE TRADEMARKS

The SAS® System is an integrated system of software providing complete control over data access, management, analysis, and presentation. Base SAS software is the foundation of the SAS System. Products within the SAS System include SAS/ACCESS®, SAS/AF®, SAS/ASSIST®, SAS/CALC®, SAS/CONNECT®, SAS/CPE®, SAS/DMI®, SAS/EIS®, SAS/ENGLISH®, SAS/ETS®, SAS/FSP®, SAS/GRAPH®, SAS/IML®, SAS/IMS-DL/I®, SAS/INSIGHT®, SAS/LAB®, SAS/OR®, SAS/PH-Clinical®, SAS/QC®, SAS/REPLAY-CICS®, SAS/SHARE®, SAS/STAT®, SAS/TOOLKIT®, SAS/DB2™, SAS/LOOKUP™, SAS/NVISION™, SAS/SQL-DS™, and SAS/TUTOR™ software. Other SAS Institute products are SYSTEM 2000® Data Management Software, with basic SYSTEM 2000, CREATE™, Multi-User™, QueX™, Screen Writer™, and CICS interface software; NeoVisuals® software; JMP®, JMP IN®, JMP SERVE®, and JMP *Design*™ software; SAS/RTERM® software the SAS/C® Compiler, and the SAS/CX® Compiler. MultiVendor Architecture™ and MVA™ are trademarks of SAS Institute Inc. SAS Institute also offers SAS Consulting®, Ambassador Select℠, and On-Site Ambassador℠ services. *Authorline*®, *SAS Communications*®, *SAS Training*®, *SAS Views*®, the SASware Ballot®, and *Observations*™ are published by SAS Institute Inc. All trademarks above are registered trademarks or trademarks of SAS Institute Inc. in the USA and other countries. ® indicates USA registration.

Other brand and product names are registered trademarks or trademarks of their respective companies.

The Institute is a private company devoted to the support and further development of its software and related services.

SAS® Macro Language Course Notes

Book code 58213 prepared 08JAN93.

ISBN 1-55544-539-X

Contents

iv

Course Description

SAS® Macro Language Course Notes serves as the text for the SAS® Macro Language course.

The SAS® Macro Language course is offered as a two-day public course in two formats: lecture and lecture/workshop. Lecture courses are taught in hotels around the United States. Lecture/workshop courses are taught at SAS Institute training centers.

The standard two-day public course can be altered for an on-site presentation, with or without workshops, at customer sites. The topics covered at an on-site course are determined by the site sponsoring the course and the Education Division of SAS Institute Inc.

Prerequisites

The SAS® Macro Language course teaches you how the SAS macro facility works and how to write programs that incorporate macro language features.

No prior knowledge of the SAS macro language is required.

However, to receive maximum benefit from the course and solve the computer exercises in the alloted time, you should have an understanding of the SAS language at the level presented in the SAS® Programming course.

Specifically, you should know how to

- prepare and submit SAS programs on your computer system

- use LIBNAME, FILENAME, TITLE, and OPTIONS statements

- use a DATA step to read from or write to a SAS data set or external data file

- use DATA step programming statements such as IF-THEN/ELSE, DO WHILE, DO UNTIL, and iterative DO

- use DATA step character functions such as SUBSTR, SCAN, INDEX, and UPCASE

- use DATA step information statements such as LENGTH and RETAIN

- use SAS data set options such as DROP=, KEEP=, and OBS=

- form subsets of data using WHERE clause syntax

- create and use SAS date values, including SAS date constants

- use base SAS procedures such as SORT, PRINT, CONTENTS, MEANS, FREQ, TABULATE, and CHART.

A basic knowledge of the SAS Display Manager System for interactive program development and debugging is desirable, but not essential.

Course Objectives

After completion of this course, you should:

Chapter 1. Introduction

- understand different applications for the SAS macro language

- understand how a SAS program is tokenized, compiled and executed

- understand how the macro processor affects program flow

Chapter 2. Using Macro Variables

- know the names of selected automatic macro variables

- know how to create your own macro variables

- know how to substitute the value of a macro variable anywhere in a program

- know how to request printing of macro variable values in the SAS log

- understand the need for macro quoting functions

Chapter 3. The DATA Step Interface

- know how to create macro variables during DATA step execution using the SYMPUT routine

- know how to create macro variables during PROC SQL execution using the INTO clause

- know how to resolve macro variables during step execution using the SYMGET function

- understand types of applications that require the functionality of the SYMGET function and SYMPUT routine

- understand how macro variables can be indirectly referenced using multiple ampersands for delayed resolution.

Course Objectives

After completion of this course, you should:

Chapter 4. Defining and Executing Macros

- know how to define and call simple macros

- know how to conditionally execute code within a macro

- understand the actions performed by the macro processor during macro compilation and execution

- know the system options available for macro debugging

- know how to interpret error and warning log messages from the macro processor

- know how to define and call macros with parameters

- understand the difference between positional and keyword parameters

- understand the difference between global and local symbol tables

- know how the macro processor decides which symbol table to use

- understand the concept of nested macros and the hierarchy of symbol tables

Chapter 5. Macro Applications

- know how to write your own messages to the SAS log during macro execution

- know how to manipulate character strings with macro functions

- know how to perform arithmetic and evaluate expressions at the macro level

- know how to repetitively execute code within a macro

- know how to create a series of macro variables for table lookup

- know how to store several values in one macro variable and how to extract all or specified values

- know how and when to use the quoting functions in applications.

Course Objectives

After completion of this course, you should:

Chapter 6. Macro Efficiencies

- know how to use the autocall facility to make macros available to a SAS program

- know how to create and use permanently stored compiled macros

- understand how system options regulate when macro variables are stored on disk rather than in memory

- know basic principles behind writing efficient macro programs.

General Conventions

This section explains the various conventions used in presenting text, SAS language syntax, and examples in this book.

Typographical Conventions

You will see several type styles in this book. The following list explains the meaning of each style:

roman   is the standard type style used for most text in this book.

UPPERCASE ROMAN
                 is used for SAS statements, variable names, and other SAS language elements when they appear in the text.

italic   defines new terms or concepts. Italic is also used for book titles when they are referenced in text.

bold   is used for emphasis within text.

`monospace`   is used for examples of SAS statements and SAS character strings. Titles, variable labels, and values of character variables are examples of character strings. Monospace is also used in text to refer to items in windows and text entered in windows.

Syntax Conventions

The general forms of SAS statements and commands shown in this book include only that part of the syntax actually taught in the course. For complete syntax, see the appropriate SAS reference guide.

Type styles have special meanings when used in the presentation of syntax in books produced by the Education Division of SAS Institute. The following list explains the style conventions:

UPPERCASE BOLD
                 identifies SAS keywords such as the names of procedures, statements, commands, functions, and macros that must be spelled exactly as shown, although not necessarily in uppercase.

General Conventions

UPPERCASE NOT BOLD
> identifies syntax that, if used, must be spelled exactly as shown, although not necessarily in uppercase.

italic
> identifies syntax that you supply. Italic is also used for generic terms that represent classes of arguments.

options
> identifies syntax specific to a particular SAS statement or command. SAS Institute reference guides use angle brackets < > to identify optional syntax in SAS statements and commands. To simplify the presentation of syntax, books produced by the Education Division do not enclose *options* in angle brackets.

vertical bar (|) indicates that you can choose one argument or value from a group. Items separated by bars are either mutually exclusive or aliases.

The following example illustrates these syntax conventions:

PROC CHART DATA = *SAS-data-set*;
    HBAR|VBAR *chart-variables / options*;
RUN;

- **PROC** and **CHART** are in uppercase bold because they are SAS keywords.

- DATA = is in uppercase to indicate that it must be spelled as shown.

- *SAS-data-set* is in italic because it represents a value that you supply. In this case, the value must be the name of a SAS data set.

- **HBAR** and **VBAR** are in uppercase bold because they are SAS keywords. They are separated by a vertical bar to indicate they are mutually exclusive; you can choose one or the other.

- *chart-variables* is in italic because it represents a value or values that you supply.

- *options* represents optional syntax specific to the PROC CHART statement.

- **RUN** is in uppercase bold because it is a SAS keyword.

1. Introduction

1.1 Overview

1.2 Program Flow

1.3 Macro Processing

1.4 Course Case Study

1.5 Exercises

1.6 Chapter Summary

1.7 Solutions and Selected Output

1.1 Overview

Purpose of the Macro Facility

The *macro facility* is a part of base SAS software that gives you programming flexibility to

- retrieve system information from the SAS Supervisor

- perform conditional or repetitive submission of SAS code

- generate data-dependent SAS statements

- communicate information between SAS steps

- create interactive windows for menuing and prompting. *Full Screen Edit*

To demonstrate features of the macro facility, this course uses data representing course registration for a company specializing in computer training.

TODAY DATE
&SASDATE

Course Overview

The SAS data set ALL contains registration information for students enrolled in data processing courses held at various locations on different dates.

Management frequently requests reports similar to the one below.

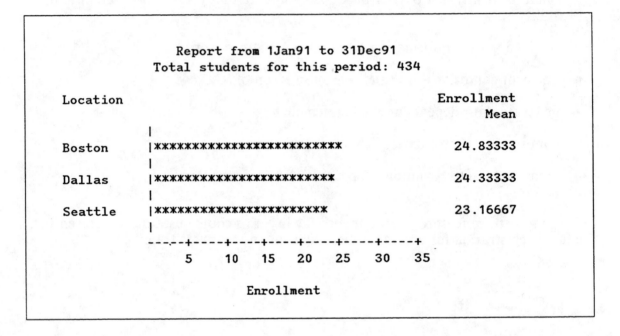

Describe the changes you would make to this program to summarize a different time period.

```
proc freq data=perm.all;
   where begin between "1Jan91"d and "31Dec91"d;
   table course*location / out=stats noprint;
proc chart data=stats;
   hbar location / sumvar=count type=mean mean
                   axis=0 to 35 by 5;
   label location='Location' count='Enrollment';
   title1 "Report from 1Jan91 to 31Dec91";
   title2 "Total students for this period: 434";
run;
```

Course Overview

Using the macro language, you can write SAS programs that are *dynamic*, or capable of self-modification.

Specifically, the macro language enables you to

- create and resolve *macro variables* anywhere in a SAS program

- write special programs (*macros*) that produce tailored SAS programs.

```
%macro attend(start,stop);
   proc freq data=perm.all;
      where begin between "&start"d and "&stop"d;
      table course*location / out=stats noprint;
   data _null_;
      retain max 0;
      set stats end=last;
      if count gt max then max=count;
      total+count;
      if last then do;
         max=5*ceil(max/5);
         call symput('total',trim(left(total)));
         call symput('max',trim(left(max)));
      end;
   proc chart data=stats;
      hbar location / sumvar=count type=mean mean
                      axis=0 to &max by 5;
      label location='Location' count='Enrollment';
      title1 "Report from &start to &stop";
      title2 "Total students for this period: &total";
   run;
%mend attend;

%attend(1Jan91,31Dec91)
```

Course Overview

This course is designed to

- help you understand how the SAS System processes SAS programs

- help you understand how macro-level programming interacts with normal program flow

- show you the syntax and coding techniques for the macro language

- demonstrate useful macro applications

- provide computer exercises for you to solve.

1.2 Program Flow

Compilation and Execution

A SAS program can be any combination of

- DATA and PROC steps

- global statements

- Screen Control Language (SCL)

- Structured Query Language (SQL)

- SAS macro language.

When you submit a program, it goes to an area of memory called the *input stack*.

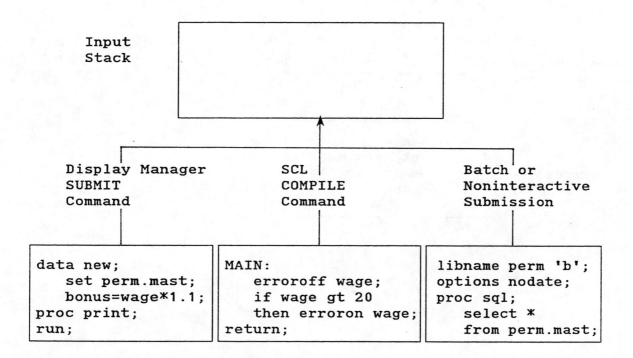

```
Input
Stack
```

```
Display Manager          SCL              Batch or
SUBMIT                   COMPILE           Noninteractive
Command                  Command           Submission
```

```
data new;            MAIN:                 libname perm 'b';
    set perm.mast;        erroroff wage;   options nodate;
    bonus=wage*1.1;      if wage gt 20     proc sql;
proc print;              then erroron wage;    select *
run;                 return;                   from perm.mast;
```

Compilation and Execution

Once SAS code is in the input stack, the SAS Supervisor

- reads the text in the input stack (left-to-right, top-to-bottom)

- routes text to the appropriate **compiler** upon demand

- suspends this activity when the compilation phase is complete

- executes the compiled code if there are no compilation errors

- repeats this process as necessary.

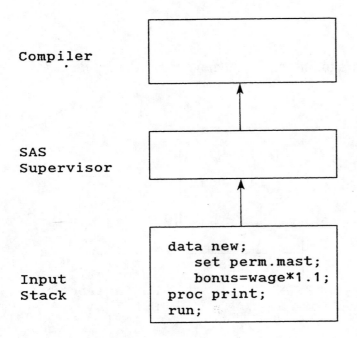

```
Compiler



SAS
Supervisor



Input        data new;
Stack            set perm.mast;
                 bonus=wage*1.1;
             proc print;
             run;
```

Tokenization

A component of the SAS Supervisor known as the *word scanner* breaks program text into fundamental units called *tokens*.

- Tokens are passed on demand to the compiler.

- The compiler requests tokens until it receives a semicolon.

- The compiler performs a syntax check on the statement.

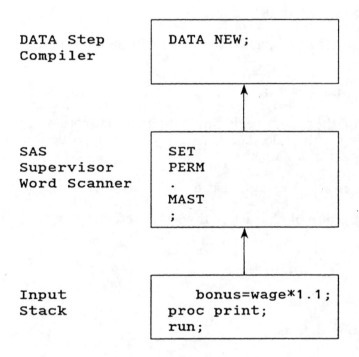

DATA Step
Compiler

```
DATA NEW;
```

SAS
Supervisor
Word Scanner

```
SET
PERM
.
MAST
;
```

Input
Stack

```
        bonus=wage*1.1;
proc print;
run;
```

How does the SAS Supervisor "know" when to stop sending statements to the DATA step compiler?

Suppose the RUN statement is omitted from the program above. How would this affect processing for

- a noninteractive submission?
- an interactive submission?

Tokenization

The word scanner recognizes four classes of tokens:

① literals   are a string of characters treated as a unit. The string is enclosed in single quotes or double quotes.

                  `'Any text'`   `"Any text"`   *200 Characters*

② numbers   are a string of digits (integers). Date, time, datetime constants and hexadecimal constants are also integer tokens.

           `23    3    100    '1jan91'd`

           are strings of digits that also include a period or E-notation (real numbers).

           `23.5    3.    .11    5e8    7.2e-4`

③ names   consist of a string of characters beginning with an underscore or letter and continuing with underscores, letters, or digits. (A period can sometimes be part of a name.)

           `infile    _n_    item3    univariate    dollar10.2`

④ special   is any character or group of characters that have reserved meaning to the compiler.

           `*  /  +  -  **  ;  $  (  )  .  &  %`

A token ends when the word scanner detects

- the beginning of another token

- a blank after a token.

The maximum length of any token is 200 characters.

Tokenization

The examples below show how the word scanner breaks statements into tokens.

The first line displays a statement in the input stack. The lines below it show the stream of tokens after word scanning.

1. Blanks are not tokens. One or more blanks only serve to separate tokens.

```
var x1-x10      z   ;

VAR
X1
-
X10
Z
;
```

2. The case of literals is preserved when the NOCAPS system option is set.

```
title 'Report for May';

TITLE
'Report for May'
;
```

3. Literals are uppercased when the CAPS system option is set.

```
title 'Report for May';

TITLE
'REPORT FOR MAY'
;
```

Tokenization

Exercise: Count the number of tokens in each statement below.

Statement	Tokens
`input a10 ssn comma11. name $30-50;`	11
`bonus=3.2*(wage-2000);`	10
`plot date*revenue='$'/vref='30jun91'd;`	12

1.3 Macro Processing

Macro Triggers

The *macro processor* is a part of the macro facility that acts upon certain token sequences detected during wordscanning:

%   followed by a name token (`%let`, for example).

&   followed by a name token (`&amt`, for example).

Each of these token sequences is called a *macro trigger*.

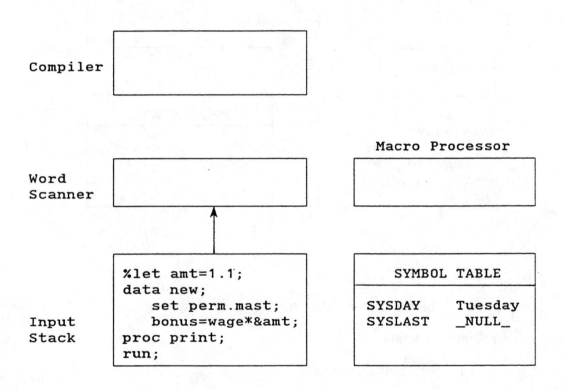

Note: The availability of the macro facility is controlled by the invocation option MACRO|NOMACRO. The default at most sites is MACRO.

How the Macro Processor Works

When a macro trigger is encountered, it is passed to the macro processor for evaluation.

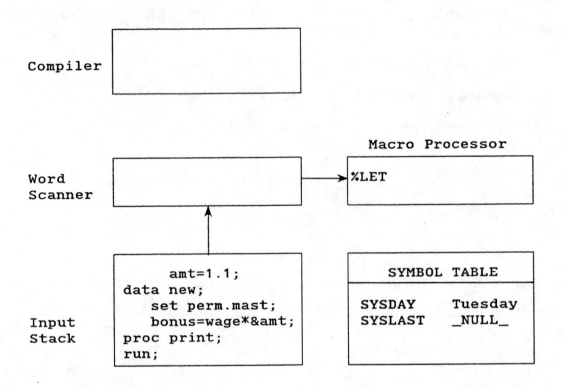

The macro processor may

- request additional tokens to complete expressions or statements

- perform some macro action

- reject a trigger as unrecognized syntax.

How the Macro Processor Works

In this case, **%LET** is the keyword of a macro statement that creates a *macro variable*. A word scanner within the macro processor requests tokens until a semicolon is encountered.

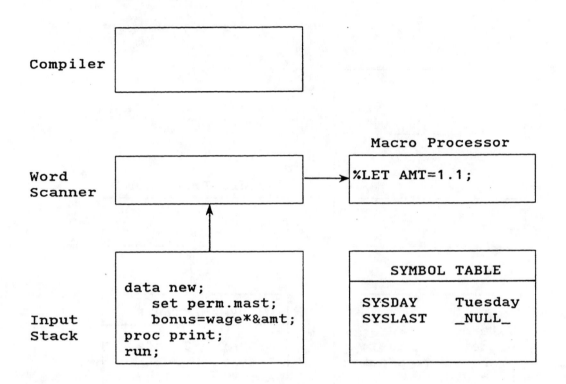

How the Macro Processor Works

The %LET statement executes.

A macro variable AMT is given the value 1.1 and stored in a memory location called a *symbol table*. Other macro variables may already exist in the symbol table.

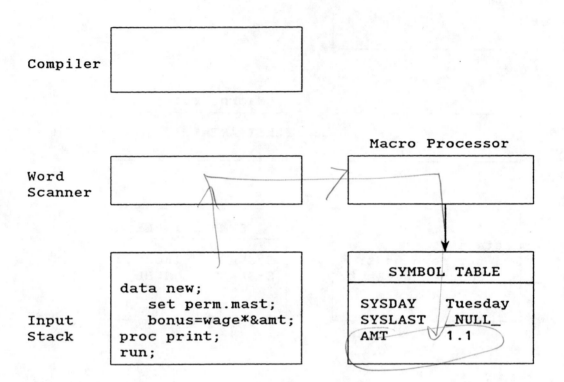

How the Macro Processor Works

Word scanning continues as usual until another macro trigger is found.

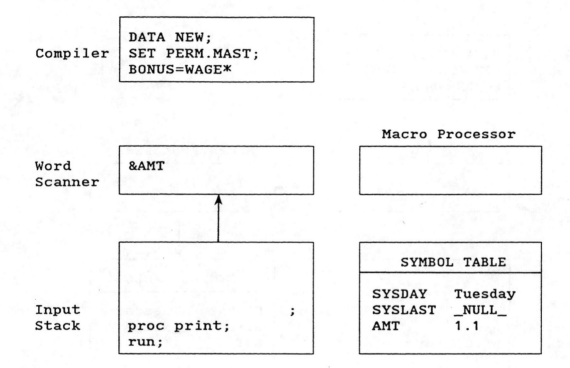

How the Macro Processor Works

The trigger &AMT is called a *macro variable reference*. The macro processor attempts to find the AMT variable in the symbol table.

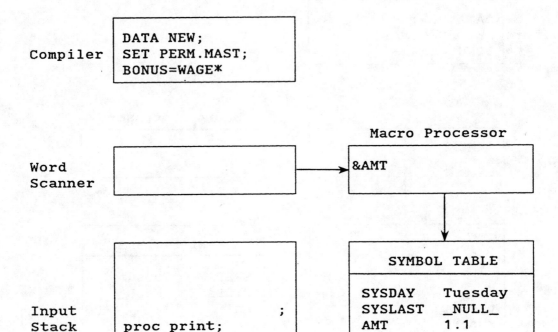

How the Macro Processor Works

If the AMT variable is found, its value is passed back to the input stack.

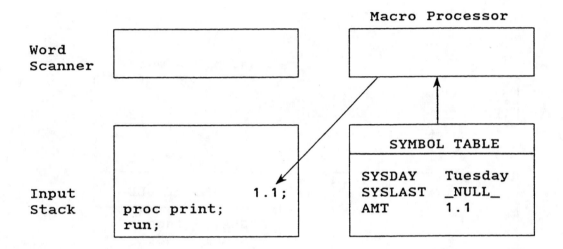

How the Macro Processor Works

Word scanning continues as usual.

When a step boundary is recognized, the DATA step compilation phase is over and execution begins.

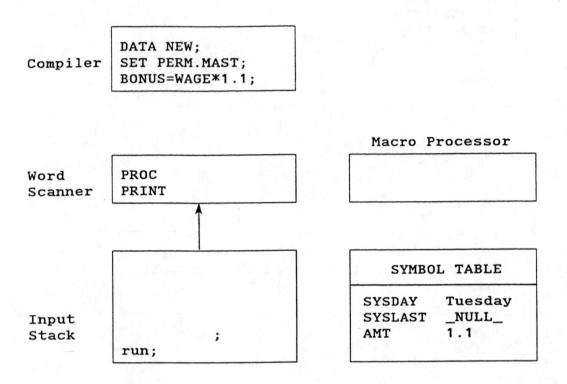

Word scanning resumes after the DATA step executes.

How the Macro Processor Works

The macro processor may write warning or error messages to the SAS log if it cannot act upon a macro trigger.

Example: Suppose the macro variable reference was coded as **&ant** instead of **&amt**.

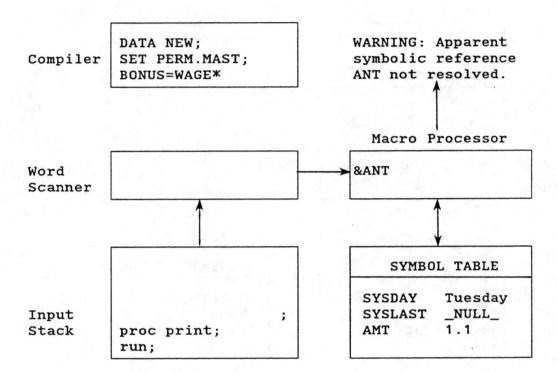

How the Macro Processor Works

If the macro processor cannot interpret the macro trigger, it passes the tokens back to the word scanner.

The DATA step compiler writes an error message to the SAS log for the statement containing &ant.

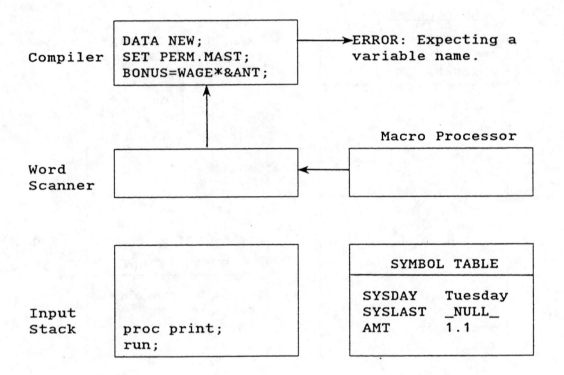

1.4 Course Case Study

A Course Registration System

Computer Educators Inc. offers short courses on computer-related subjects.

The company presents its courses in cities (Boston, Dallas, and Seattle) around the United States.

The company is developing a registration and reporting system.

Data for 1991 are documented on the following pages.

SAS Data Set	Description
COURSES	Contains information about courses with one observation per course.
SCHEDULE	Contains information about each course offered with one observation per course at a particular location and date.
STUDENTS	Contains information about students with one observation per student.
REGISTER	Contains information about students registered for a specific course with one observation per student for a particular course.
ALL	Contains a data view linking all data files with one observation per student per course.

These data sets are stored in a SAS data library with a libref of PERM:

TSO: `libname perm 'edu.macro.sasdata' disp=shr;`

CMS: `libname perm 'a';`

Under directory-based systems such as VMS, OS/2, and UNIX, all course files are stored in a subdirectory named MACRO.

The COURSES Data Set

```
                    Contents of PERM.COURSES Data Set

Data Set Name: PERM.COURSES          Observations:            6
Member Type:   DATA                  Variables:               4
Engine:        V606                  Indexes:                 0
Created:       7:53 Fri, Nov 15, 1991  Observation Length:    45
Last Modified: 7:53 Fri, Nov 15, 1991  Deleted Observations:  0
Data Set Type:                       Compressed:             NO


               -----Variables Ordered by Position-----

#  Variable  Type  Len  Pos  Format     Informat   Label
-----------------------------------------------------------------
1  COURSE    Char    4    0  .          .          Course Code
2  TITLE     Char   25    4  .          .          Description
3  DAYS      Num     8   29  1.         1.         Course Length
4  FEE       Num     8   37  DOLLAR5.   DOLLAR5.   Course Fee
```

```
                   Listing of PERM.COURSES Data Set

    OBS    COURSE    TITLE                        DAYS      FEE

     1     C001      Basic Telecommunications       3     $795
     2     C002      Structured Query Language      4     $1150
     3     C003      Local Area Networks            3     $650
     4     C004      Database Design                2     $375
     5     C005      Artificial Intelligence        2     $400
     6     C006      Computer Aided Design          5     $1600
```

The SCHEDULE Data Set

```
                  Contents of PERM.SCHEDULE Data Set

Data Set Name: PERM.SCHEDULE          Observations:          18
Member Type:   DATA                   Variables:             5
Engine:        V606                   Indexes:               0
Created:       7:54 Fri, Nov 15, 1991 Observation Length:    55
Last Modified: 7:54 Fri, Nov 15, 1991 Deleted Observations:  0
Data Set Type:                        Compressed:            NO


                -----Variables Ordered by Position-----

#  Variable  Type  Len  Pos  Format     Informat   Label
-------------------------------------------------------------------
1  CRSNUM    Num    8    0   2.         2.         Course Number
2  COURSE    Char   4    8   .          .          Course Code
3  LOCATION  Char  15   12   .          .          Location
4  BEGIN     Num    8   27   DATE7.     DATE7.     Begin
5  TEACHER   Char  20   35   .          .          Instructor
```

The SCHEDULE Data Set

Listing of PERM.SCHEDULE Data Set

OBS	CRSNUM	COURSE	LOCATION	BEGIN	TEACHER
1	1	C001	Dallas	04FEB91	Hallis, Dr. George
2	2	C002	Dallas	04MAR91	Wickam, Dr. Alice
3	3	C003	Dallas	11MAR91	Forest, Mr. Peter
4	4	C004	Dallas	25MAR91	Tally, Ms. Julia
5	5	C005	Dallas	08APR91	Hallis, Dr. George
6	6	C006	Dallas	06MAY91	Berthan, Ms. Judy
7	7	C001	Seattle	10JUN91	Hallis, Dr. George
8	8	C002	Seattle	17JUN91	Wickam, Dr. Alice
9	9	C003	Seattle	08JUL91	Forest, Mr. Peter
10	10	C004	Seattle	22JUL91	Tally, Ms. Julia
11	11	C005	Seattle	29JUL91	Tally, Ms. Julia
12	12	C006	Seattle	12AUG91	Berthan, Ms. Judy
13	13	C001	Boston	09SEP91	Hallis, Dr. George
14	14	C002	Boston	16SEP91	Wickam, Dr. Alice
15	15	C003	Boston	23SEP91	Forest, Mr. Peter
16	16	C004	Boston	07OCT91	Tally, Ms. Julia
17	17	C005	Boston	21OCT91	Hallis, Dr. George
18	18	C006	Boston	11NOV91	Berthan, Ms. Judy

The STUDENTS Data Set

```
                Contents of PERM.STUDENTS Data Set

Data Set Name: PERM.STUDENTS          Observations:         207
Member Type:   DATA                   Variables:            3
Engine:        V606                   Indexes:              0
Created:       7:52 Fri, Nov 15, 1991 Observation Length:   85
Last Modified: 7:52 Fri, Nov 15, 1991 Deleted Observations: 0
Data Set Type:                        Compressed:           NO


            -----Variables Ordered by Position-----


#  Variable  Type  Len  Pos  Format     Informat   Label
------------------------------------------------------------
1  NAME      Char  25   0    .          .          Student Name
2  COMPANY   Char  40   25   .          .          Company
3  CITYST    Char  20   65   .          .          City,State
```

```
            Partial Listing of PERM.STUDENTS Data Set

OBS        NAME              COMPANY                 CITYST

  1   Abramson, Ms. Andrea  Eastman Developers    Deerfield, IL
  2   Alamutu, Ms. Julie    Reston Railway        Chicago, IL
  3   Albritton, Mr. Bryan  Special Services      Oak Brook, IL
  4   Allen, Ms. Denise     Department of Defense Bethesda, MD
  5   Amigo, Mr. Bill       Assoc. of Realtors    Chicago, IL
```

The REGISTER Data Set

```
                 Contents of PERM.REGISTER Data Set

Data Set Name: PERM.REGISTER          Observations:          434
Member Type:   DATA                   Variables:             3
Engine:        V606                   Indexes:               0
Created:       7:53 Fri, Nov 15, 1991 Observation Length:    34
Last Modified: 7:53 Fri, Nov 15, 1991 Deleted Observations:  0
Data Set Type:                        Compressed:            NO


                -----Variables Ordered by Position-----

 #   Variable  Type  Len  Pos  Format      Informat    Label
---------------------------------------------------------------------
 1   NAME      Char   25   0   .           .           Student Name
 2   CRSNUM    Num     8  25   2.          2.          Course Number
 3   PAID      Char    1  33   .           .           Paid Status
```

```
              Partial Listing of PERM.REGISTER Data Set

      OBS            NAME              CRSNUM    PAID

       1     Albritton, Mr. Bryan        1       Y
       2     Amigo, Mr. Bill             1       N
       3     Chodnoff, Mr. Norman        1       Y
       4     Clark, Mr. Rich             1       Y
       5     Crace, Mr. Ron              1       Y
```

The ALL Data View

The program used to create the SAS data view is shown below.

```
proc sql;
   create view perm.all as
   select students.name,schedule.crsnum,paid,
          courses.course,location,begin,
          teacher,title,days,fee,company,cityst
     from perm.schedule,perm.courses,
          perm.register,perm.students
    where schedule.course=courses.course and
          schedule.crsnum=register.crsnum and
          students.name=register.name;
```

```
                    Contents of PERM.ALL View

Data Set Name: PERM.ALL              Observations:          .
Member Type:   VIEW                  Variables:             12
Engine:        SQLVIEW               Indexes:               0
Created:       14:08 Fri, Nov 15, 91 Observation Length:    196
Last Modified: 14:08 Fri, Nov 15, 91 Deleted Observations:  0
Data Set Type:                       Compressed:            NO


              -----Variables Ordered by Position-----


   # Variable Type Len Pos Format    Informat  Label
  ---------------------------------------------------------------
     1 NAME     Char 25   0 .          .         Student Name
     2 CRSNUM   Num   8  32 2.         2.        Course Number
     3 PAID     Char  1  40 .          .         Paid Status
     4 COURSE   Char  4  41 .          ..        Course Code
     5 LOCATION Char 15  45 .          .         Location
     6 BEGIN    Num   8  64 DATE7.     DATE7.    Begin
     7 TEACHER  Char 20  72 .          .         Instructor
     8 TITLE    Char 25  92 .          .         Description
     9 DAYS     Num   8 120 1.         1.        Course Length
    10 FEE      Num   8 128 DOLLAR5.   DOLLAR5.  Course Fee
    11 COMPANY  Char 40 136 .          .         Company
    12 CITYST   Char 20 176 .          .         City,State
```

The ALL Data View

Character Variables - (Mixed Case)

Partial Listing of PERM.ALL View

OBS	NAME	CRSNUM	PAID	COURSE	LOCATION
1	Abramson, Ms. Andrea	10	Y	C004	Seattle
2	Abramson, Ms. Andrea	6	N	C006	Dallas
3	Alamutu, Ms. Julie	14	N	C002	Boston
4	Albritton, Mr. Bryan	1	Y	C001	Dallas
5	Albritton, Mr. Bryan	5	Y	C005	Dallas

OBS	BEGIN	TEACHER	TITLE
1	22JUL91	Tally, Ms. Julia	Database Design
2	06MAY91	Berthan, Ms. Judy	Computer Aided Design
3	16SEP91	Wickam, Dr. Alice	Structured Query Language
4	04FEB91	Hallis, Dr. George	Basic Telecommunications
5	08APR91	Hallis, Dr. George	Artificial Intelligence

OBS	DAYS	FEE	COMPANY	CITYST
1	2	$375	Eastman Developers	Deerfield, IL
2	5	$1600	Eastman Developers	Deerfield, IL
3	4	$1150	Reston Railway	Chicago, IL
4	3	$795	Special Services	Oak Brook, IL
5	2	$400	Special Services	Oak Brook, IL

1.5 Exercises

Ref pages
23-30

From your student account, you have access to program files.

TSO: This is a PDS containing existing programs and should be used to store programs you create.

userid.WORKSHOP.SASCODE   (fileref = PGM)

CMS: All course files are on your A-disk.

Other: All course files are in a subdirectory named MACRO.

1.1   Compilation and Execution of SAS Programs

Issue the SAS command to begin a SAS Display Manager System session. Issue the KEYS command to identify the function key that issues the SUBMIT command.

Execute the program below by typing one token in the PROGRAM EDITOR window text area and pressing the SUBMIT function key, typing the next token, pressing the SUBMIT function key, and so on.

```
proc        (submit)
options     (submit)
;           (submit)
proc        (submit)
print       (submit)
;           (submit)
run         (submit)
;           (submit)
```

After submitting which token do you notice that the PROC OPTIONS step executes? ____;_____

After submitting which token do you get an error message in the LOG window? __PRINT_____

After submitting which token do you get a note indicating that the SAS Supervisor stopped processing the step? __;_____

Exercises

1.2   Tokenizing a SAS Program

Issue the INCLUDE command to bring the program file C1EX2 into the PROGRAM EDITOR window.

TSO: Command = = = > `inc pgm(c1ex2)`

CMS: Command = = = > `inc c1ex2`

```
options nosource nonotes ;
data  _null_ ;
   start = " &systime "t ;
   now = time( );
   cost = ( now - start ) * .02 ;
   put / / + 9 'Your session cost is' cost dollar8.2;
run;
options source notes ;
```

a.   Edit the program so that all nonessential blanks are removed within each statement. Submit the program and check the SAS log. Recall and edit the program until it runs without a syntax error.

b.   Edit the program so that each token appears on a separate line.

(Hint: Open the KEYS window and assign `:TS` to the function key currently defined as RFIND. The TS line command splits a line where the cursor rests. Assign `:TC` to the function key currently defined as RCHANGE. The TC line command connects two lines where the cursor rests.)

Submit the program and check the SAS log. If you have a syntax error, you may have to "reconnect" text so it is treated as one token.

Recall and edit the program until it produces output similar to the previous exercise.

Exercises

[handwritten: LIBNAME PERM 'SYS3.SAS6.WORKSHOP.SASDATA';]

1.3   Tokenizing a Macro Trigger

The program below is stored in a file named C1EX3. It creates a listing of students enrolled in a specific course.

```
proc print data=perm.all label noobs n;
   where crsnum=&num;
   var name company cityst;
   options nodate number pagno=1;
   title "Enrollment for Course &num";
run;
```

a.   Submit a **%INCLUDE** statement to execute the C1EX3 code directly without including it in the PROGRAM EDITOR window:

TSO: Command = = = > **submit**

   00001 **%inc pgm(c1ex3);**

CMS: Command = = = > **submit**

   00001 **%inc c1ex3;**

[handwritten: %INCLUDE 'SYS3.SAS6.WORKSHOP. SASCODE(C1EX3)'; Points to + Submits C1EX3 (Pgm)]

You should see a message in the SAS log indicating the macro variable NUM is not defined.

b.   Refer to the documentation for the PERM.SCHEDULE data set. What is the CRSNUM value for the **C002** course taught in **Seattle** on **17JUN91**? ____8____ *[handwritten: Crsc(8)]*

Submit a **%LET** statement that assigns the appropriate CRSNUM value for the Seattle course to the macro variable NUM. *[handwritten: %Let NUM=8;]*

Recall the **%INCLUDE** statement and submit it. The program should create a report for the requested course.

Submit another **%LET** statement to specify a different value for NUM (use any value 1 to 18). Recall the **%INCLUDE** statement and submit it. You should get a different course roster.

[handwritten margin note: error to correct. %Let = /]

1.6 Chapter Summary

The macro facility enables you to generate repetitive SAS code, generate data-dependent SAS statements and steps, perform conditional execution of DATA and PROC steps, pass information between steps, and extract information from the SAS Supervisor. These features provide you with the capability of creating very sophisticated self-modifying programs.

In order to properly use the macro facility, you must understand how it interacts with the processing of a SAS program. Macro syntax in a program is intercepted by the word scanner prior to reaching the SAS compiler. The macro processor manipulates the character strings it receives to construct SAS statements, parts of SAS statements, constants, or text and passes them to the SAS Supervisor to be compiled and executed in the traditional manner. The macro language serves as a dynamic editor for SAS programs.

The objectives of the course are to present the syntax of the macro language, to further explain how the macro facility works, and to present the syntax and coding techniques needed to design, write, and debug macro systems. These objectives are met in part by examples and exercises that build on problems from the case study described in this chapter.

1.7 Solutions and Selected Output

1.1   Compilation and Execution of SAS Programs

The PROC OPTIONS step executes after the word scanner reads the `print` token.

The error message appears after the PROC PRINT statement is compiled. (The semicolon after the `print` token.)

The note appears after the RUN statement is compiled. (The semicolon after the `run` token.)

1.2   Tokenizing a SAS Program

a.

```
options nosource nonotes;
data _null_;
start="&systime"t;
now=time();
cost=(now-start)*.02;
put//+9'Your session cost is'cost dollar8.2;
run;
options source notes;
```

Solutions and Selected Output

1.2   Tokenizing a SAS Program (continued)

    b.

```
options
nonotes
nosource
;
data
_null_
;
start
=
"&systime"t
;
now
=
time
(
)
;
cost
=
(
now
-
start
)
*
.02
;
```

(Continued on next page.)

Solutions and Selected Output

1.2   Tokenizing a SAS Program (continued)

b.

```
put
/
/
+
9
'Your session cost is'
cost
dollar8.2
;
run
;
options
notes
source
;
```

1.3   Tokenizing a Macro Trigger

a.

Partial SAS Log

```
5          +     where crsnum=&num;

                        _
                        22
WARNING: Apparent symbolic reference NUM not resolved.
ERROR: Syntax error while parsing WHERE clause.
WARNING: Apparent symbolic reference NUM not resolved.
```

Solutions and Selected Output

1.3   Tokenizing a Macro Trigger (continued)

   b.

```
%let num=8;
```

Partial SAS Log

```
NOTE: The PROCEDURE PRINT printed pages 1-2.
```

Last Page of Output

```
                        Enrollment for Course 8                        2

        Student Name                Company

        Ramsey, Ms. Kathleen        Pacific Solid State Corp.
        Shipman, Ms. Jan            Southern Edison Co.
        Sulzbach, Mr. Bill          Sailbest Ships
        Woods, Mr. Joseph           Federal Landmarks

        City,State

        Seattle, WA
        Sacramento, CA
        San Diego, CA
        Washington, DC


                            N = 20
```

2. Using Macro Variables

2.1 Basic Concepts

Global Variables

Whenever a SAS program is executed noninteractively or at the beginning of an interactive SAS session, a **global** symbol table is created and initialized with **automatic** or system-defined macro variables.

You can also create **user-defined** global macro variables with the %LET statement:

```
%let city=Dallas;
%let date=4Feb91;
%let amount=795;
```

```
                  GLOBAL  SYMBOL  TABLE

                        .
                        .
Automatic         SYSTIME    09:47
Variables         SYSVER     6.07
                        .
                        .
User-defined
Variables         CITY       Dallas
                  DATE       4Feb91
                  AMOUNT     795
```

Note: User-defined macro variables can also be stored in **local** symbol tables. These tables are discussed in Chapter 4.

Referencing a Macro Variable

To substitute the value of a macro variable in your program, you must reference it.

A macro variable reference

- is made by preceding the macro variable name with an **ampersand** (&)

- causes the macro processor to search for the named variable and return its value if the variable exists.

```
GLOBAL SYMBOL TABLE

CITY       Dallas
DATE       4Feb91
AMOUNT     795
```

```
    where fee>&amount;
```

generates

```
    WHERE FEE>795;
```

Referencing a Macro Variable

If you need to reference a macro variable within a literal, enclose the literal in double quotes.

```
GLOBAL SYMBOL TABLE

CITY      Dallas
DATE      4Feb91
AMOUNT    795
```

```
     where cityst contains "&city";
```

generates

```
WHERE CITYST CONTAINS "Dallas";
```

IF BEGIN = "&DATE"D;

```
     where cityst contains '&city';
```

DOES NOT WORK

generates

```
WHERE CITYST CONTAINS '&city';
```

IF BEGIN = "4FEB91"D;

Note: The word scanner continues to tokenize literals enclosed in double quotes, but not literals enclosed in single quotes.

Referencing a Macro Variable

If you reference a nonexistent macro variable, a warning message is printed in the SAS log.

```
┌─────────────────────────────┐
│ GLOBAL SYMBOL TABLE         │
├─────────────────────────────┤
│ CITY      Dallas            │
│ DATE      4Feb91            │
│ AMOUNT    795               │
└─────────────────────────────┘
```

```
where fee>&cost;

WARNING: Apparent symbolic reference COST not resolved.
```

If you supply an invalid name for a macro variable, an error message is printed in the SAS log.

```
where cityst contains "&citystate";

ERROR: Symbolic variable name CITYSTATE must be 8 or fewer
       characters long.
```

The SYMBOLGEN Option

To monitor the value that is substituted when a macro variable is referenced, you specify the SYMBOLGEN system option:

```
options symbolgen;
```

This system option displays the results of resolving macro variable references in the SAS log.

```
GLOBAL SYMBOL TABLE

CITY       Dallas
DATE       4Feb91
AMOUNT     795
```

Examples:

```
where fee>&amount;
SYMBOLGEN: Macro variable AMOUNT resolves to 795


where cityst contains "&city";
SYMBOLGEN: Macro variable CITY resolves to Dallas


where cityst contains '&city';
```

No message is displayed. Why?

Note: The default option setting is NOSYMBOLGEN.

2.2 Automatic Macro Variables

Variables Defined by the System

System-defined or **automatic** macro variables are created by the SAS Supervisor.

These variables

- are created at SAS invocation

- are global (always available)

- are usually assigned values by the SAS Supervisor

- can be assigned values by the user in some cases.

Some automatic macro variables have fixed values that are set at SAS invocation:

Name	Value
SYSDATE	date of SAS invocation
SYSDAY	day of the week of SAS invocation
SYSTIME	time of SAS invocation
SYSENV	FORE (interactive execution) BACK (noninteractive or batch execution)
SYSSCP	abbreviation for the operating system being used such as OS, CMS, VMS, PC DOS, HP 300, or OS2
SYSVER	release of the SAS System being used
SYSJOBID	identifier of current SAS session or batch job
	mainframe systems: the identifier is the userid or job name
	other systems: the identifier is the process ID (PID)

Variables Defined by the System

Example: Substitute system information in footnotes for a report.

```
libname perm 'edu.macro.sasdata' disp=shr; * MVS;
options nodate nonumber;
footnote1 "Report created &systime &sysday, &sysdate";
footnote2 "on an &sysscp machine using Version &sysver";
footnote3 "by &sysjobid";
title "1991 REVENUES FOR DALLAS TRAINING CENTER";
proc tabulate data=perm.all(keep=location title fee) noseps;
   where upcase(location)="DALLAS";
   class title;
   var fee;
   table title=' ' all='TOTALS',
         fee=' '*(n*f=3. sum*f=dollar10.)
         / rts=30 box='COURSE';
run;
```

```
            1991 REVENUES FOR DALLAS TRAINING CENTER


        -------------------------------------------------
        |COURSE                       | N |   SUM      |
        |-----------------------------+---+-----------|
        |Artificial Intelligence      | 25|  $10,000|
        |Basic Telecommunications     | 23|  $18,285|
        |Computer Aided Design        | 27|  $43,200|
        |Database Design              | 27|  $10,125|
        |Local Area Networks          | 20|  $13,000|
        |Structured Query Language    | 24|  $27,600|
        |TOTALS                       |146| $122,210|
        -------------------------------------------------


            Report created 16:18 Tuesday, 21JAN92
            on an OS machine using Version 6.07
                       by EDU023
```

Variables Defined by the System

Some automatic macro variables have values that automatically change based on submitted SAS statements:

%LET SYSRC=____; [handwritten]

(=0) Good [handwritten]

Name	Value
SYSERR	return code set by the last DATA or PROC step
SYSRC *	return code set by the last operating system command
SYSLIBRC *	return code set by the last LIBNAME statement
SYSFILRC *	return code set by the last FILENAME statement
SYSLAST *	name of most recently created SAS data set in the form *libref.name*. If no data set has been created, the value is _NULL_.
SYSPARM *	text specified at program invocation.

Note: Most automatic variables are read only. Some (*) can be updated with programming statements.

Variables Defined by the System

Typical values of selected automatic macro variables are shown below.

```
┌─────────────────────────────┐
│ GLOBAL SYMBOL TABLE         │
├─────────────────────────────┤
│  SYSDATE      30SEP91        │
│  SYSDAY       Monday         │
│  SYSTIME      15:45          │
│  SYSENV       FORE           │
│  SYSSCP       OS             │
│  SYSVER       6.07           │
│  SYSJOBID     EDU001         │
│  SYSERR       0              │
│  SYSRC        0              │
│  SYSLIBRC     0              │
│  SYSFILRC     0              │
│  SYSLAST      _NULL_         │
│  SYSPARM                     │
└─────────────────────────────┘
```

Note: The values of the macro variables SYSDATE and SYSTIME are character strings, **not** SAS date or time values.

The macro variables SYSERR, SYSLIBRC, and SYSFILRC resolve to **0** when the SAS statements they monitor are error free. Nonzero values imply a warning, a syntax error, or execution error.

Values assigned to the macro variable SYSRC are host dependent.

Applications for Automatic Variables

Possible applications for automatic macro variables:

SYSDATE	Check the current date to execute programs on certain days of the month. Substitute the value in a TITLE statement.
SYSDAY	Check the value to run a given job on a certain day of the week.
SYSENV	Check the execution mode before submitting code that requires interactive (foreground) processing.
SYSSCP	Check the operating system in order to execute appropriate system commands.
SYSVER	Check for the release of the SAS System being used before executing a job with newer features.
SYSJOBID	Check who is currently executing the job to restrict certain processing or issue commands specific to a user.
SYSERR	Check the return code from a SAS procedure and abort the job if the return code is nonzero.
SYSRC	Check the return code of any system command before continuing with the job.
SYSLIBRC	Check the return code from a LIBNAME statement before attempting to access permanent SAS data sets.
SYSFILRC	Check the return code from a FILENAME statement before attempting to access a non-SAS file.

Note: Checking the value of a macro variable requires conditional logic (%IF-%THEN and %ELSE statements) in a SAS macro program, which is discussed in Chapter 4.

The SYSPARM Macro Variable

You can supply a value for the SYSPARM macro variable at SAS invocation using the SYSPARM= system option.

This is useful for tailoring a production program without modifying its source code.

Example: Use one program to create a revenue report for any training center. Supply the name of the center as part of a noninteractive execution.

The production program is shown below:

```
libname perm 'edu.macro.sasdata' disp=shr; * MVS;
title "1991 REVENUES FOR &sysparm TRAINING CENTER";
options nodate nonumber formchar='               ';
proc tabulate data=perm.all(keep=location title fee);
   where upcase(location)="&sysparm";
   class title;
   var fee;
   table title=' ' all='TOTALS',
         fee=' '*(n*f=3. sum*f=dollar10.)
         / rts=30 box='COURSE';
run;
```

This is overvariable example

Multiple is ok

To assign the value **DALLAS** to the SYSPARM macro variable, specify the SYSPARM= system option as follows:

MVS BATCH
```
//         EXEC SAS,OPTIONS='SYSPARM=DALLAS'
//SYSIN DD DSN=program-name,DISP=SHR
```

TSO   `sas input('''program-name''') opt('sysparm=DALLAS')`

CMS   `sas program-name (sysparm=DALLAS)`

VMS   `sas/sysparm=DALLAS program-name`

OS/2 and UNIX
`          sas program-name -sysparm DALLAS`

The SYSPARM Macro Variable

Output for SYSPARM Value of DALLAS

```
           1991 REVENUES FOR DALLAS TRAINING CENTER

           COURSE                      N     SUM

           Artificial Intelligence     25    $10,000

           Basic Telecommunications    23    $18,285

           Computer Aided Design       27    $43,200

           Database Design             27    $10,125

           Local Area Networks         20    $13,000

           Structured Query Language   24    $27,600

           TOTALS                      146   $122,210
```

2.3 User-defined Macro Variables

The %LET Statement

The **%LET** statement enables you to define a macro variable and assign it a value.

General form of the %LET statement:

> **%LET** *variable* = *value*;

Rules for the %LET statement:

- *variable* can be any name following the SAS naming convention
- *value* can be any string:
  - the case of *value* is preserved
  - maximum length is 32K characters   *steps (multiple)*
  - minimum length is 0 characters (**null value**)   *%LET NAME=;*
  - numeric tokens are stored as character strings   *' NAME'*
  - mathematical expressions are not evaluated   *=1+2; = 1+2 = NOT 3 hAS*
  - quotes bounding literals are stored as part of *value*
- leading and trailing blanks are removed from *value* before the assignment is made
- if *variable* already exists in the symbol table, *value* replaces the current value
- if either *variable* or *value* contains a macro trigger, the trigger is evaluated before the assignment is made.

Note: In Release 6.07, the macro facility stores long values on disk. See Chapter 6 for details.

%LET Statement Examples

Use the rules on the previous page to determine the value of the following macro variables.

```
%let name=    Ed Norton  ;

%let name2='  Ed Norton  ';

%let title="Joan's Report";

%let start=;

%let total=0;

%let sum=3+4;

%let total=&total+&sum;

%let x=varlist;

%let &x=name age height;
```

Symbol Table

VARIABLE	VALUE
NAME	ED NORTON
NAME2	' ED NORTON '
TITLE	"JOAN'S REPORT"
START	_NULL_
TOTAL	0
SUM	3+4
TOTAL	0 + 3+4
X	VARLIST
VARLIST	NAME AGE HEIGHT

%LET Statement Examples

Example: Assign the value **DALLAS** to the macro variable SITE. Use the macro
variable to control program output.

```
%let site=DALLAS;
libname perm 'edu.macro.sasdata' disp=shr; * MVS;
title "1991 REVENUES FOR &site TRAINING CENTER";
options nodate nonumber formchar='              ';
proc tabulate data=perm.all(keep=location title fee);
   where upcase(location)="&site";
   class title;
   var fee;
   table title=' ' all='TOTALS',
         fee=' '*(n*f=3. sum*f=dollar10.)
         / rts=30 box='COURSE';
run;
```

```
                1991 REVENUES FOR DALLAS TRAINING CENTER


        COURSE                         N      SUM

        Artificial Intelligence       25    $10,000

        Basic Telecommunications      23    $18,285

        Computer Aided Design         27    $43,200

        Database Design               27    $10,125

        Local Area Networks           20    $13,000

        Structured Query Language     24    $27,600

        TOTALS                       146   $122,210
```

2.4 Macro Variable References

Building Tokens

You can reference macro variables anywhere in your program.

Some applications may require placing a macro variable reference adjacent to leading or trailing text

> . . . `text`*`&variable`* `text` . . .
>
> . . . `text` *`&variable`*`text` . . .
>
> . . . `text`*`&variable`*`text` . . .

or referencing adjacent macro variables

> . . . *`&variable&variable`* . . .

in order to build a new token.

Combining Macro Variables with Text

You can place text immediately before a macro variable reference to build a new token.

Example: Data sets are stored in a SAS data library with the following naming convention:

> Yyear-month

year   can be 88, 89, 90, 91, and so on.

month   can be JAN, FEB, MAR, and so on.

Write a program that uses a macro variable to build the month portion of the SAS data set name.

```
* MONTH should be three characters;

%let month=jan;

proc chart data=perm.y90&month;
   hbar week / sumvar=sale;
proc plot data=perm.y90&month;
   plot sale*day;
run;
```

generates

```
PROC CHART DATA=PERM.Y90JAN;
   HBAR WEEK / SUMVAR=SALE;
PROC PLOT DATA=PERM.Y90JAN;
   PLOT SALE*DAY;
RUN;
```

Combining Macro Variables with Text

You can reference macro variables that have no blanks between them to build new tokens.

Example: Modify the previous program to allow both the month and the year to be substituted.

```
* YEAR should be 2 digits;
* MONTH should be three characters;

%let year=90;
%let month=jan;

proc chart data=perm.y&year&month;
   hbar week / sumvar=sale;
proc plot data=perm.y&year&month;
   plot sale*day;
run;
```

generates

```
PROC CHART DATA=PERM.Y90JAN;
   HBAR WEEK / SUMVAR=SALE;
PROC PLOT DATA=PERM.Y90JAN;
   PLOT SALE*DAY;
RUN;
```

Combining Macro Variables with Text

You can place text immediately after a macro variable reference if it does not change the name of the macro variable.

Example: Modify the previous program to substitute the name of an analysis variable.

```
* YEAR should be 2 digits;
* MONTH should be three characters;
* VAR should be an existing numeric variable;

%let year=90;
%let month=jan;
%let var=sale;

proc chart data=perm.y&year&month;
    hbar week / sumvar=&var;
proc plot data=perm.y&year&month;
    plot &var*day;
run;
```

generates

```
PROC CHART DATA=PERM.Y90JAN;
    HBAR WEEK / SUMVAR=SALE;
PROC PLOT DATA=PERM.Y90JAN;
    PLOT SALE*DAY;
RUN;
```

Combining Macro Variables with Text

Example: Modify the previous program to allow a graphics or nongraphics
procedure.

```
* GRAPHICS should be null or G;
* YEAR should be 2 digits;
* MONTH should be three characters;
* VAR should be an existing numeric variable;

%let graphics=g;
%let year=90;
%let month=jan;
%let var=sale;

proc &graphicschart data=perm.y&year&month;
    hbar week / sumvar=&var;
proc &graphicsplot data=perm.y&year&month;
    plot &var*day;
run;
```

What is wrong with this program?

Macro Variable Name Delimiter

The word scanner recognizes the end of a macro variable name when it encounters a character that cannot be part of the name token.

A **period** (.) is a special character that is treated as part of the macro variable reference and does not appear when the macro variable is resolved.

Example: Correct the resolution problem in the previous example.

```
%let graphics=g;
%let year=90;
%let month=jan;
%let var=sale;

proc &graphics.chart data=perm.y&year&month;
     .
     .
     .
```

delimiter

If these SAS statements are executed, the

- word scanner treats `&graphics.` as the reference

- value of the macro variable GRAPHICS is returned to the input stack

- word scanner processes `gchart` as one token.

The SAS compiler receives:

```
PROC GCHART DATA=PERM.Y90JAN;
     .
     .
     .
```

Macro Variable Name Delimiter

Example: Modify the previous program to include a macro variable used to define
the libref.

```
%let lib=perm;
%let graphics=g;
%let year=90;
%let month=jan;
%let var=sale;

libname &lib 'edc.macro.sasdata';

proc &graphics.chart data=&lib.y&year&month;
   .
   .
   .
```

What is the problem this time?

delimiter

Macro Variable Name Delimiter

The statements

```
%let lib=perm;
%let graphics=G;
%let year=90;
%let month=jan;

libname &lib 'edc.macro.sasdata';

proc &graphics.chart data=&lib.y&year&month;
```

send this statement to the SAS compiler:

```
PROC GCHART DATA=PERMY90JAN;
```

The period after `&lib` is interpreted as a delimiter.

Use another period after the delimiter period to supply the needed token.

delimiter————————————text

```
proc &graphics.chart data=&lib..y&year&month;
```

The compiler receives:

```
PROC GCHART DATA=PERM.Y90JAN;
```

2.5 Quoting in the Macro Facility

What Is Quoting?

The SAS language uses matched pairs of double or single quotes to distinguish character constants from names.

The quotes are not stored as part of the token they define.

```
data one;
    var='TEXT';
proc print;
    title "Joan's Report";
run;
```

VAR is stored as a 4-byte variable with a value of TEXT. If TEXT were not enclosed in quotes, it would be treated as a variable name.

The title that appears does not contain the outer matched quotes.

What Is Quoting?

The macro facility uses & to reference its variables. Paired quotes are not needed to designate character constants.

```
                                       ┌─────────────────────────┐
                                       │     Symbol Table        │
                                       ├─────────────────────────┤
%let mvar1=TEXT;          ─────────►   │  MVAR1      TEXT        │
%let mvar2='TEXT';        ─────────►   │  MVAR2      'TEXT'      │
                                       └─────────────────────────┘
```

What is the type, length, and value of each DATA step variable below?

	NAME	TYPE	LENGTH	VALUE
`data one;`				
`    text='HI';`	TEXT	$\$$	2	HI
`    var1=&mvar1;`	VAR1	$\$$	2	HI
`    var2="&mvar1";` *"TEXT"*;	VAR2	$\$$	4	"TEXT
`    var3='&mvar1';`	VAR3	$\$$	6	------
`    var4=&mvar2;` *'TEXT');*	VAR4	$\$$	4	TEXT
`    var5="&mvar2";`	VAR5	$\$$	6	'TEXT'
`    var6='&mvar2';`	VAR6	$\$$	6	-----
`run;`				

VAR5 = " 'TEXT' ";

Tip: For greater flexibility, do not store the quotes as part of a macro variable value. It is easier to supply quotes in your program as needed instead of working around a value that has quotes in it. The following programs are equivalent:

```
%let month=MAY;                    %let month='MAY';
title "REPORT FOR &month";         title "REPORT FOR "&month;
proc print;                        proc print;
   where month="&month";              where month=&month;
run;                               run;
```

Need for Macro Quoting

Suppose you want to store one or more SAS statements in a macro variable.

```
options symbolgen;

%let prog=data new; x=1; run;

&prog
proc print;
run;
```

How do you explain the processing reported in this SAS log?

```
1               options symbolgen;
2
3               %let prog=data new; x=1; run;
                               ─
                              180
ERROR 180-322: Statement is not valid or it is used out of proper
               order.

SYMBOLGEN:  Macro variable PROG resolves to data new
4
5               &prog
6               proc print;
7               run;

NOTE: SAS set option OBS=0 and will continue to check statements.
      This may cause NOTE: No observations in data set.
NOTE: The data set WORK.NEW has 0 observations and 0 variables.
NOTE: The data set WORK.PROC has 0 observations and 0 variables.
NOTE: The data set WORK.PRINT has 0 observations and 0 variables.

ERROR: Errors printed on page 1.
```

In some applications you need to mask the meaning of text you want to assign to a macro variable.

You can use *macro quoting functions* to remove the normal syntactic meaning of tokens.

The %STR Function

The **%STR** function is used to alter (*quote*) tokens so the macro processor does not interpret them as macro-level syntax.

General form of the **%STR** function:

%STR(*argument*)

argument   can be any combination of text and macro triggers.

This macro function

- removes the normal meaning of a semicolon and other special tokens that appear as constant text

- allows macro triggers to work normally

- preserves leading and trailing blanks in its argument.

Other special tokens include:

```
,
+    -    *    /    **
<         =         >         &         |         ¬         <=        >=        ¬=
LT        EQ        GT        AND       OR        NOT       LE        GE        NE
```

Note: The macro language contains several quoting functions. For example, the %NRSTR function performs the same quoting function as **%STR**, except it also quotes macro triggers. This quoting function and others are discussed in Chapter 5.

The %STR Function

Example: Use the **%STR** function to store one or more SAS statements as the value of a macro variable.

Method One: Quote all text.

```
%let prog=%str(data new; x=1; run;);
```

Method Two: Quote only the semicolons.

```
%let prog=data new%str(;) x=1%str(;) run%str(;);
```

Method Three: Create a macro variable with a quoted value.

```
%let s=%str(;);
%let prog=data new&s x=1&s run&s;
```

The %STR Function

Example: Suppose you want to assign text containing an apostrophe to a macro
variable.

```
options symbolgen;

%let text=Our Site's Options;
proc options;
title "&text";
run;
```

SAS Log

```
1          options symbolgen;
2
3          %let text=Our Site's Options;
WARNING: The current word or quoted string has become more than
         200 characters long.  You may have unbalanced
         quotation marks.
4          proc options;
5          title "&text";
6          run;
```

The **%STR** function can also be used to quote tokens that normally occur in pairs:

```
    '    "      )      (
```

To perform this quoting, you must precede any of the above tokens with a percent
sign within the **%STR** function argument.

```
%let text=%str(Our Site%'s Options);

%let text=Our Site%str(%')s Options;
```

The value of TEXT is **Our Site's Options** in both cases.

2.6 Exercises

2.1   Using and Defining Macro Variables

a.   Issue the SAS command to begin a display manager session. Include the C2EX1 program into the PROGRAM EDITOR window.

    TSO: Command = = = > `inc pgm(c2ex1)`
    CMS: Command = = = > `inc c2ex1`

The program shown below creates a listing of all courses a given student (or group of students) has taken.

```
proc sort data=perm.all out=select;
   by name;
   where name contains 'Babbit';
proc print data=select noobs label uniform;
   by name company;
   pageby name;
   var title begin location teacher;
   title  'Courses Taken by Selected Students:';
   title2 'Those with Babbit in Their Name';
   options nodate nonumber nocenter;
run;
```

Add a FOOTNOTE statement to the PROC PRINT step that supplies today's date (use an automatic macro variable) using the following text:

    Report Created on *date*

Submit the program and examine the output it creates.

b.   Recall the program and change the name pattern in the WHERE statement and TITLE2 statement to `Ba` and resubmit. Examine the output. Clear the OUTPUT window.

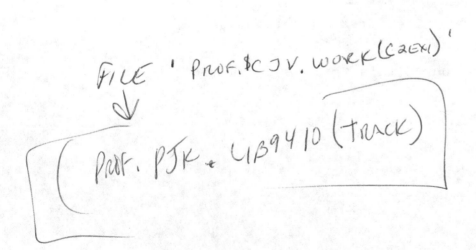

Exercises

2.1   Using and Defining Macro Variables (continued)

c.   Modify the program so the two occurrences of **Ba** are replaced by references to the macro variable PATTERN. Precede the program with a %LET statement to assign the value **Ba** to PATTERN. Submit the program. It should produce the same output as before. File your program as TRACK when it works properly.

```
TSO: Command = = = > file pgm(track)
CMS: Command = = = > file track
```

d.   Create a listing of all courses attended by a student with the last name of **O'Savio**. (Hint: You must remove the meaning of the apostrophe before you assign a value to PATTERN.)

2.2   Creating Macro Variable References (Optional)

a.   Include the program C2EX2 shown below into the PROGRAM EDITOR window.

```
title;
proc sql;
    select location,n(location) label='Count'
        from perm.schedule,perm.register
        where schedule.crsnum=register.crsnum
        group by location;
quit;
```

table 1   *table 2*

Submit the program. The SELECT statement creates a listing from two SAS data sets (tables) that are merged (joined) by a common variable CRSNUM. The GROUP BY clause reduces the listing to distinct values of LOCATION. The N function counts the number of observations that are within distinct values of the GROUP BY variable.

%LET

Exercises

2.2   Creating Macro Variable References (Optional) (continued)

b.   Modify the program so it contains references to the following macro variables:

TABLE1   second-level name of one input data set

TABLE2   second-level name of the other input data set

JOINVAR   name of variable common to both input data sets

FREQVAR   name of the GROUP BY variable.

Precede the program with %LET statements that initialize these macro variables to the values currently in the program. Submit the program and compare the listing with the one created earlier. They should be identical.

c.   Recall the program and change the values of the macro variables to create a listing from the STUDENTS and REGISTER data sets that shows the distribution of the CITYST variable. The two data sets share the NAME variable.

2.7 Chapter Summary

A global symbol table is created at the beginning of every SAS job. Several automatic macro variables are placed in this table and assigned values. Examples of these variables are SYSDATE, SYSPARM, and SYSJOBID. You can create your own macro variables with a **%LET** statement anywhere in a SAS program. Macro variables can also be stored in local symbol tables when a SAS macro program is executing.

Macro variables store text. You can assign no text (null value) to a variable as well as very long text strings (there is no 200 character limit). To assign text containing special characters (semicolons, for example) to a macro variable, you use a macro quoting function (%STR, for example) to remove the normal meaning of the characters.

To resolve a macro variable, you place an ampersand in front of the variable name. Constant text can be placed immediately in front of or behind a macro variable reference. If the text behind the reference might change the name of the variable, you use a period after the name to delimit the name. This period is not part of the resolved value.

The SYMBOLGEN system option is used to print the current value of any referenced macro variable in the SAS log.

General form of the **%LET** statement:

    %LET *variable* = *value*;

General form of the **%STR** function:

    %STR(*argument*)

2.8 Solutions and Selected Output

2.1   Using and Defining Macro Variables

a.

```
footnote "Report Created on &sysdate";
```

b.

```
proc sort data=perm.all out=select;
   by name;
   where name contains 'Ba';
proc print data=select noobs label uniform;
   by name company;
   pageby name;
   var title begin location teacher;
   title  'Courses Taken by Selected Students:';
   title2 'Those with Ba in Their Name';
   options nodate nonumber nocenter;
   footnote "Report Created on &sysdate";
run;
```

c.

```
%let pattern=Ba;
proc sort data=perm.all out=select;
   by name;
   where name contains "&pattern";
proc print data=select noobs label uniform;
   by name company;
   pageby name;
   var title begin location teacher;
   title  'Courses Taken by Selected Students:';
   title2 "Those with &pattern in Their Name";
   options nodate nonumber nocenter;
   footnote "Report Created on &sysdate";
run;
```

Solutions and Selected Output

2.1   Using and Defining Macro Variables (continued)

d.   Modify the **%LET** statement as shown below. (Either **%LET** statement is correct.) The rest of the program is unchanged.

```
%let pattern=%str(O%'Savio);
%let pattern=O%str(%')Savio;
```

2.2   Creating Macro Variable References (Optional)

b.

```
%let table1=schedule;
%let table2=register;
%let joinvar=crsnum;
%let freqvar=location;
title;
proc sql;
   select &freqvar,n(&freqvar) label='Count'
      from perm.&table1,perm.&table2
      where &table1..&joinvar=&table2..&joinvar
      group by &freqvar;
quit;
```

```
               The SAS System

          Location           Count
          -------------------------
          Boston               149
          Dallas               146
          Seattle              139
```

Solutions and Selected Output

2.2   Creating Macro Variable References (Optional) (continued)

c.

```
%let table1=register;
%let table2=students;
%let joinvar=name;
%let freqvar=cityst;
title;
proc sql;
   select &freqvar,n(&freqvar) label='Count'
      from perm.&table1,perm.&table2
      where &table1..&joinvar=&table2..&joinvar
      group by &freqvar;
quit;
```

3. The DATA Step Interface

3.1 The SYMPUT Routine

3.2 The SYMGET Function

3.3 The SQL Interface (Optional)

3.4 The SCL Interface (Optional)

3.5 Exercises

3.6 Chapter Summary

3.7 Solutions and Selected Output

3.1 The SYMPUT Routine

Introduction

In many applications, you need to create macro variables that are assigned values based on

- data values stored in files (SAS data sets or external files)

- programming logic or computed values.

Example: Create a report listing students enrolled in a specific course. Include a footnote indicating whether any student fees are due.

[handwritten: %let FOOT1 = 'SF Due';]
[handwritten: %let FOOT2 = 'All Paid';]

```
options symbolgen;
%let crsnum=3;
data revenue;
   set perm.all end=final;
   where crsnum=&crsnum;
   total+1;
   if paid='Y' then paidup+1;
   if final then do;
      put total= paidup=;
      if paidup<total then do;
         %let foot=Some Fees Due;
      end;
      else do;
         %let foot=All Students Paid;
      end;
   end;
proc print data=revenue;
   var name company paid;
   title "Paid Status for Course &crsnum";
   footnote "&foot";
run;
```

[handwritten annotations: TOTAL; PAID UP; &FOOT1 replaces &FOOT2]

Examine the output and SAS log on the next two pages. Why did the two %LET statements in the DATA step not have the desired effect?

Introduction

Program Output

```
                    Paid Status for Course 3

  OBS NAME                        COMPANY                        PAID

    1 Bills, Ms. Paulette         Reston Railway                  Y
    2 Chevarley, Ms. Arlene       Motor Communications            N
    3 Clough, Ms. Patti           Reston Railway                  N
    4 Crace, Mr. Ron              Von Crump Seafood               Y
    5 Davis, Mr. Bruce            Semi;Conductor                  Y
    6 Elsins, Ms. Marisa F.       SSS Inc.                        N
    7 Gandy, Dr. David            Paralegal Assoc.                Y
    8 Gash, Ms. Hedy              QA Information Systems Center    Y
    9 Haubold, Ms. Ann            Reston Railway                  Y
   10 Hudock, Ms. Cathy           So. Cal. Medical Center         Y
   11 Kimble, Mr. John            Alforone Chemical               N
   12 Kochen, Mr. Dennis          Reston Railway                  Y
   13 Larocque, Mr. Bret          Physicians IPA                  Y
   14 Licht, Mr. Bryan            SII                             Y
   15 McKnight, Ms. Maureen E.    Federated Bank                  Y
   16 Scannell, Ms. Robin         Amberly Corp.                   N
   17 Seitz, Mr. Adam             Lomax Services                  Y
   18 Smith, Ms. Jan              Reston Railway                  N
   19 Sulzbach, Mr. Bill          Sailbest Ships                  Y
   20 Williams, Mr. Gene          Snowing Petroleum               Y

                        All Students Paid
```

Introduction

Partial SAS Log

```
2          options symbolgen;
3          %let crsnum=3;
4          data revenue;
5             set perm.all end=final;
6             where crsnum=&crsnum;

SYMBOLGEN:  Macro variable CRSNUM resolves to 3
7             total+1;
8             if paid='Y' then paidup+1;
9             if final then do;
10               put total= paidup=;
11               if paidup<total then do;
12                  %let foot=Some Fees Due;
13               end;
14               else do;
15                  %let foot=All Students Paid;
16               end;
17            end;

TOTAL=20 PAIDUP=14
NOTE: The data set WORK.REVENUE has 20 observations and 14
      variables.

18         proc print data=revenue;
19            var name company paid;
20

SYMBOLGEN:  Macro variable CRSNUM resolves to 3
20            title "Paid Status for Course &crsnum";
SYMBOLGEN:  Macro variable FOOT resolves to All Students Paid
21            footnote "&foot";
22         run;
```

The SYMPUT Routine

Whenever you submit a DATA step, a *program data vector (PDV)* is created in memory. This storage area is used by the DATA step to manipulate the current observation.

All variables in the PDV are defined during step compilation:

- variables explicitly defined using statements such as LENGTH and INPUT

- variables implicitly defined using statements such as SET and MERGE

- automatic variables such as _N_ and _ERROR_

- special variables such as FIRST.*by-variable* and LAST.*by-variable*

The values stored in the PDV can change during DATA step execution.

The DATA step offers functions and routines that allow transfer of information between an **executing** DATA step and the macro processor.

You can use the SYMPUT routine to assign a value available to the DATA step to a macro variable.

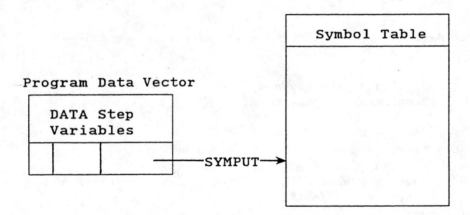

Because macro variables store character values only, any numeric DATA step value must be converted to a character string before it can be assigned to a macro variable by the SYMPUT routine.

The SYMPUT Routine

The SYMPUT routine creates a macro variable and assigns it a value.

General form of the SYMPUT routine:

CALL SYMPUT(*macro-variable*,*text*);

macro-variable   is assigned the character value of *text*.

You can specify *macro-variable* or *text* as a

- literal

- DATA step variable

- DATA step expression

These combinations are illustrated on the following pages.

Note: If *macro-variable* already exists, the value of *text* replaces the old value.

The SYMPUT Routine with Literals

Both arguments of the SYMPUT routine can be literals:

CALL SYMPUT(*'macro-variable'*,*'text'*);

This form of the SYMPUT routine assigns the *text* within the quotes to *macro-variable*.

Example: Conditionally assign a value to a macro variable FOOT based on DATA step values. Reference this macro variable later in the program.

```
%let crsnum=3;
data revenue;
   set perm.all end=final;
   where crsnum=&crsnum;
   total+1;
   if paid='Y' then paidup+1;
   if final then do;
      if paidup<total then
            call symput('foot','Some Fees Due');
      else call symput('foot','All Students Paid');
   end;
proc print data=revenue;
   var name company paid;
   title "Paid Status for Course &crsnum";
   footnote "&foot";
run;
```

The value assigned to FOOT is either `Some Fees Due` or `All Students Paid`.

The SYMPUT Routine with Literals

Program Output

```
                    Paid Status for Course 3

    OBS NAME                      COMPANY                    PAID

      1 Bills, Ms. Paulette       Reston Railway              Y
      2 Chevarley, Ms. Arlene     Motor Communications        N
      3 Clough, Ms. Patti         Reston Railway              N
      4 Crace, Mr. Ron            Von Crump Seafood           Y
      5 Davis, Mr. Bruce          Semi;Conductor              Y
      6 Elsins, Ms. Marisa F.     SSS Inc.                    N
      7 Gandy, Dr. David          Paralegal Assoc.            Y
      8 Gash, Ms. Hedy            QA Information Systems Center Y
      9 Haubold, Ms. Ann          Reston Railway              Y
     10 Hudock, Ms. Cathy         So. Cal. Medical Center     Y
     11 Kimble, Mr. John          Alforone Chemical           N
     12 Kochen, Mr. Dennis        Reston Railway              Y
     13 Larocque, Mr. Bret        Physicians IPA              Y
     14 Licht, Mr. Bryan          SII                         Y
     15 McKnight, Ms. Maureen E.  Federated Bank              Y
     16 Scannell, Ms. Robin       Amberly Corp.               N
     17 Seitz, Mr. Adam           Lomax Services              Y
     18 Smith, Ms. Jan            Reston Railway              N
     19 Sulzbach, Mr. Bill        Sailbest Ships              Y
     20 Williams, Mr. Gene        Snowing Petroleum           Y

                        Some Fees Due
```

The SYMPUT Routine with Literals

Change the value of the macro variable CRSNUM to 18. The output is shown below.

```
                    Paid Status for Course 18

  OBS NAME                      COMPANY                    PAID

    1 Amigo, Mr. Bill           Assoc. of Realtors          Y
    2 Babbitt, Mr. Bill         National Credit Corp.       Y
    3 Bates, Ms. Ellen          Reston Railway              Y
    4 Benincasa, Ms. Elizabeth  Hospital Nurses Association  Y
    5 Blair, Mr. Paul           Federal Lankmarks           Y
    6 Cookson, Ms. Michelle     Log Chemical                Y
    7 Dyer, Ms. Debra           Cetadyne Technologies       Y
    8 Elsins, Ms. Marisa F.     SSS Inc.                    Y
    9 Guay, Ms. Suzanne         U.S. Foreign Trade Assoc.   Y
   10 Huels, Ms. Mary Frances   Basic Home Services         Y
   11 McCoy, Ms. Gail           Crossbow of California      Y
   12 Parker, Mr. Robert        SMASH Hardware Inc.         Y
   13 Pickens, Ms. Margaret     Semi;Conductor              Y
   14 Ross, Ms. Cathy           So. Cal. Medical Center     Y
   15 Stebel, Mr. Thomas C.     Roam Publishers             Y
   16 Strah, Ms. Sonia          California Dept. of Insurance Y
   17 Turner, Ms. Barbara       Gravely Finance Center      Y
   18 Walls, Mr. Curtis         Southern Edison Co.         Y
   19 Ziegler, Mr. David        US Express Corp.            Y


                       All Students Paid
```

SYMPUT with a Literal and Variable

The form of the SYMPUT routine shown below creates the macro variable named by *macro-variable* and assigns it the current value of *DATA-step-variable*.

CALL SYMPUT(*'macro-variable'*,*DATA-step-variable*);

When a DATA step variable is used as the second argument,

- a maximum of 200 characters can be assigned to the receiving macro variable

- any leading or trailing blanks that are part of the DATA step variable's value are stored in the macro variable.

Example: Create macro variables from the DATA step variables PAIDUP, TOTAL, and TITLE. Resolve these macro variables later in the program.

```
%let crsnum=3;
data revenue;
   set perm.all end=final;
   where crsnum=&crsnum;
   total+1;
   if paid='Y' then paidup+1;
   if final then do;
      call symput('numpaid',paidup);
      call symput('numstu',total);
      call symput('crsname',title);
   end;
proc print data=revenue noobs;
   var name company paid;
   title "Fee Status for &crsname (#&crsnum)";
   footnote "Note: &numpaid Paid out of &numstu Students";
run;
```

Note: If the DATA step variable is numeric, its current value is converted to a right-aligned character value using the BEST12. format before the SYMPUT routine executes.

SYMPUT with a Literal and Variable

Program Output

```
            Fee Status for Local Area Networks        (#3)

    NAME                    COMPANY                        PAID

    Bills, Ms. Paulette     Reston Railway                  Y
    Chevarley, Ms. Arlene   Motor Communications            N
    Clough, Ms. Patti       Reston Railway                  N
    Crace, Mr. Ron          Von Crump Seafood               Y
    Davis, Mr. Bruce        Semi;Conductor                  Y
    Elsins, Ms. Marisa F.   SSS Inc.                        N
    Gandy, Dr. David        Paralegal Assoc.                Y
    Gash, Ms. Hedy          QA Information Systems Center   Y
    Haubold, Ms. Ann        Reston Railway                  Y
    Hudock, Ms. Cathy       So. Cal. Medical Center         Y
    Kimble, Mr. John        Alforone Chemical               N
    Kochen, Mr. Dennis      Reston Railway                  Y
    Larocque, Mr. Bret      Physicians IPA                  Y
    Licht, Mr. Bryan        SII                             Y
    McKnight, Ms. Maureen E. Federated Bank                 Y
    Scannell, Ms. Robin     Amberly Corp.                   N
    Seitz, Mr. Adam         Lomax Services                  Y
    Smith, Ms. Jan          Reston Railway                  N
    Sulzbach, Mr. Bill      Sailbest Ships                  Y
    Williams, Mr. Gene      Snowing Petroleum               Y

        Note:          14 Paid out of        20 Students
```

SYMPUT with a Literal and Variable

Before the SYMPUT routine executes, you might want to use DATA step functions to

- left-align character strings created by numeric-to-character conversions

- remove extraneous leading and trailing blanks.

Example: Remove leading blanks from the macro variables NUMSTU and NUMPAID. Remove trailing blanks from CRSNAME.

```
data revenue;
   set perm.all end=final;
   where crsnum=&crsnum;
   total+1;
   if paid='Y' then paidup+1;
   if final then do;
      call symput('numpaid',trim(left(paidup)));
      call symput('numstu',trim(left(total)));
      call symput('crsname',trim(title));
   end;
proc print data=revenue noobs;
   var name company paid;
   title "Fee Status for &crsname (#&crsnum)";
   footnote "Note: &numpaid Paid out of &numstu Students";
run;
```

get rid of Blanks

Note: The LEFT function removes leading blanks.

The TRIM function removes trailing blanks. Leading blanks are unaffected.

Using a numeric argument with a character function causes automatic conversion to character. Messages appear in the SAS log.

SYMPUT with a Literal and Variable

Program Output

```
            Fee Status for Local Area Networks (#3)

    NAME                     COMPANY                    PAID

    Bills, Ms. Paulette      Reston Railway              Y
    Chevarley, Ms. Arlene    Motor Communications        N
    Clough, Ms. Patti        Reston Railway              N
    Crace, Mr. Ron           Von Crump Seafood           Y
    Davis, Mr. Bruce         Semi;Conductor              Y
    Elsins, Ms. Marisa F.    SSS Inc.                    N
    Gandy, Dr. David         Paralegal Assoc.            Y
    Gash, Ms. Hedy           QA Information Systems Center  Y
    Haubold, Ms. Ann         Reston Railway              Y
    Hudock, Ms. Cathy        So. Cal. Medical Center     Y
    Kimble, Mr. John         Alforone Chemical           N
    Kochen, Mr. Dennis       Reston Railway              Y
    Larocque, Mr. Bret       Physicians IPA              Y
    Licht, Mr. Bryan         SII                         Y
    McKnight, Ms. Maureen E. Federated Bank              Y
    Scannell, Ms. Robin      Amberly Corp.               N
    Seitz, Mr. Adam          Lomax Services              Y
    Smith, Ms. Jan           Reston Railway              N
    Sulzbach, Mr. Bill       Sailbest Ships              Y
    Williams, Mr. Gene       Snowing Petroleum           Y

         Note: 14 Paid out of 20 Students
```

SYMPUT with DATA Step Expressions

You can also use a DATA step expression to specify the value assigned to the macro variable.

    CALL SYMPUT(*'macro-variable'*,*expression*);

When you use a DATA step *expression* as the second argument,

- its current value is evaluated to a character constant (numeric expressions are automatically converted to character)

- you can assign a maximum of 200 characters to the receiving macro variable

- any leading or trailing blanks that are part of the expression are stored in the macro variable.

SYMPUT with DATA Step Expressions

Example: Format the value of the numeric variable BEGIN with the
MMDDYY8. format and assign it to the macro variable DATE.
Format the result of an expression involving TOTAL and PAIDUP as
a dollar amount and assign it to the macro variable DUE.

```
%let crsnum=3;
data revenue;
   set perm.all end=final;
   where crsnum=&crsnum;
   total+1;
   if paid='Y' then paidup+1;
   if final then do;
      call symput('crsname',trim(title));
      call symput('date',put(begin,mmddyy8.));
      call symput('due',
           trim(left(put(fee*(total-paidup),dollar10.))));
   end;
proc print data=revenue;
   var name company paid;
   title "Fee Status for &crsname (#&crsnum) Held &date";
   footnote "Note: &due in Unpaid Fees";
run;
```

Note: The PUT function returns the character string formed by writing a value
with a specified format. The format determines the width of the resulting
string and whether it is right or left aligned.

General form of the PUT function:

PUT(*source, format*)

source   is a constant, variable, or expression (numeric or
character).

format   is any SAS format or user-defined format.

SYMPUT with DATA Step Expressions

Program Output

```
         Fee Status for Local Area Networks (#3) Held 03/11/91

  OBS NAME                    COMPANY                       PAID

    1 Bills, Ms. Paulette     Reston Railway                 Y
    2 Chevarley, Ms. Arlene   Motor Communications           N
    3 Clough, Ms. Patti       Reston Railway                 N
    4 Crace, Mr. Ron          Von Crump Seafood              Y
    5 Davis, Mr. Bruce        Semi;Conductor                 Y
    6 Elsins, Ms. Marisa F.   SSS Inc.                       N
    7 Gandy, Dr. David        Paralegal Assoc.               Y
    8 Gash, Ms. Hedy          QA Information Systems Center  Y
    9 Haubold, Ms. Ann        Reston Railway                 Y
   10 Hudock, Ms. Cathy       So. Cal. Medical Center        Y
   11 Kimble, Mr. John        Alforone Chemical              N
   12 Kochen, Mr. Dennis      Reston Railway                 Y
   13 Larocque, Mr. Bret      Physicians IPA                 Y
   14 Licht, Mr. Bryan        SII                            Y
   15 McKnight, Ms. Maureen E. Federated Bank                Y
   16 Scannell, Ms. Robin     Amberly Corp.                  N
   17 Seitz, Mr. Adam         Lomax Services                 Y
   18 Smith, Ms. Jan          Reston Railway                 N
   19 Sulzbach, Mr. Bill      Sailbest Ships                 Y
   20 Williams, Mr. Gene      Snowing Petroleum              Y

             Note: $3,900 in Unpaid Fees
```

Computing Statistics for Later Use

Recall the program presented at the beginning of the course.

```
proc freq data=perm.all;
    where begin between "1Jan91"d and "31Dec91"d;
    table course*location / out=stats noprint;
proc chart data=stats;
    hbar location / sumvar=count type=mean mean
                    axis=0 to 35 by 5;
    label location='Location' count='Enrollment';
    title1 "Report from 1Jan91 to 31Dec91";
    title2 "Total students for this period: 434";
run;
```

This version of the program only requires the maintenance of the %LET statements to dynamically generate reports for different periods.

```
%let start=1Jan91;
%let stop=31Dec91;

proc freq data=perm.all;
    where begin between "&start"d and "&stop"d;
    table course*location / out=stats noprint;
data _null_;
    retain max 0;
    set stats end=last;
    if count gt max then max=count;
    total+count;
    if last then do;
        max=5*ceil(max/5);
        call symput('total',trim(left(total)));
        call symput('max',trim(left(max)));
    end;
proc chart data=stats;
    hbar location / sumvar=count type=mean mean
                    axis=0 to &max by 5;
    label location='Location' count='Enrollment';
    title1 "Report from &start to &stop";
    title2 "Total students for this period: &total";
run;
```

Computing Statistics for Later Use

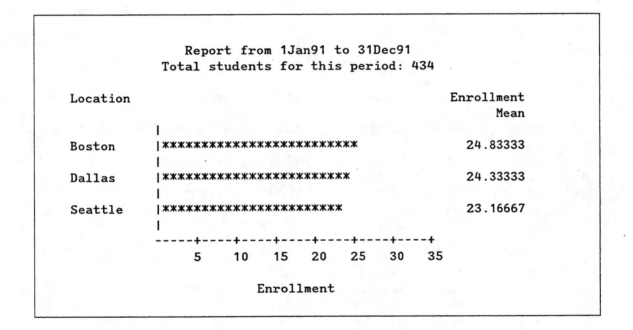

```
                 Partial Listing of STATS Data Set

        OBS    COURSE    LOCATION    COUNT    PERCENT

         1     C001      Boston       28      6.45161
         2     C001      Dallas       23      5.29954
         3     C001      Seattle      18      4.14747
         4     C002      Boston       33      7.60369
         5     C002      Dallas       24      5.52995
```

```
                    Report from 1Jan91 to 31Dec91
                    Total students for this period: 434

   Location                                         Enrollment
                                                       Mean

                  |
   Boston         |****************************       24.83333
                  |
   Dallas         |**************************         24.33333
                  |
   Seattle        |************************           23.16667
                  |
                  -----+----+----+----+----+----+----+
                       5   10   15   20   25   30   35

                            Enrollment
```

Note: You can use this technique in SAS/GRAPH applications to dynamically scale axes.

Most statistical procedures create output data sets containing computed values. A DATA step can read these data sets and SYMPUT routines can store the computed values in macro variables. The macro variables can be used for designating reference lines or titling information.

Creating Multiple Macro Variables with SYMPUT

Recall these data sets from the case study:

```
                    Listing of PERM.COURSES Data Set

   √ COURSE     TITLE                        DAYS      FEE

      C001      Basic Telecommunications       3      $795
      C002      Structured Query Language      4      $1150
      C003      Local Area Networks            3      $650
      C004      Database Design                2      $375
      C005      Artificial Intelligence        2      $400
      C006      Computer Aided Design          5      $1600
```

```
            Partial Listing of PERM.SCHEDULE Data Set

   CRSNUM   √ COURSE    LOCATION     BEGIN        TEACHER

      1        C001     Dallas      04FEB91    Hallis, Dr. George
      2        C002     Dallas      04MAR91    Wickam, Dr. Alice
      3        C003     Dallas      11MAR91    Forest, Mr. Peter
      4        C004     Dallas      25MAR91    Tally, Ms. Julia
      5        C005     Dallas      08APR91    Hallis, Dr. George
      6        C006     Dallas      06MAY91    Berthan, Ms. Judy
      7        C001     Seattle     10JUN91    Hallis, Dr. George
      8        C002     Seattle     17JUN91    Wickam, Dr. Alice
      9        C003     Seattle     08JUL91    Forest, Mr. Peter
     10        C004     Seattle     22JUL91    Tally, Ms. Julia
     11        C005     Seattle     29JUL91    Tally, Ms. Julia
     12        C006     Seattle     12AUG91    Berthan, Ms. Judy
     13        C001     Boston      09SEP91    Hallis, Dr. George
     14        C002     Boston      16SEP91    Wickam, Dr. Alice
     15        C003     Boston      23SEP91    Forest, Mr. Peter
```

Creating Multiple Macro Variables with SYMPUT

Example: Write a program that lists all offerings of a given course. Create listings
for courses C005 and C002. Use the course description in a title. The
listing program is stored in a file and is assigned a fileref of LOOKUP1.

Fileref = LOOKUP1

```
data _null_;
   set perm.courses;
   where course="&crsid";
   call symput('title',trim(title));
run;
proc print data=perm.schedule noobs label;
   where course="&crsid";
   var location begin teacher;
   title1 "Schedule for &title";
   options nodate nonumber;
run;
```

This program uses the LOOKUP1 program to generate the two reports.

```
libname perm 'edc.macro.sasdata' disp=shr;
filename lookup1 'edc.macro.sascode(lookup1)';
options symbolgen source2;
%let crsid=C005;
%include lookup1;
%let crsid=C002;
%include lookup1;
```

Note: The %INCLUDE statement can also be coded as follows:

```
%include 'edc.macro.sascode(lookup1)';
```

Creating Multiple Macro Variables with SYMPUT

The first DATA step is executed to create the macro variable TITLE. The output is shown below.

```
            Schedule for Artificial Intelligence

        Location      Begin         Instructor

        Dallas       08APR91    Hallis, Dr. George
        Seattle      29JUL91    Tally, Ms. Julia
        Boston       21OCT91    Hallis, Dr. George
```

The next DATA step is executed to update the TITLE variable with a different value for the next report.

```
            Schedule for Structured Query Language

        Location      Begin         Instructor

        Dallas       04MAR91    Wickam, Dr. Alice
        Seattle      17JUN91    Wickam, Dr. Alice
        Boston       16SEP91    Wickam, Dr. Alice
```

Creating Multiple Macro Variables with SYMPUT

Instead of executing separate DATA steps to update the same macro variable, you could create related macro variables in one DATA step.

Advantages include

- efficiency

- reduced coding.

Use the SYMPUT routine with DATA step expressions for both arguments to create multiple macro variables.

CALL SYMPUT(*expression1*,*expression2*);

expression1   evaluates to a character value that is a valid macro variable name. This value should change each time you want to create another macro variable.

expression2   is the value you want to assign to a specific macro variable.

Creating Multiple Macro Variables with SYMPUT

Example: Create one macro variable for each value of the DATA step variable
COURSE. Assign the corresponding value of TITLE to each macro
variable.

SAS Log for the DATA Step

```
2              data _null_;
3                  set perm.courses;
4                  call symput(course,trim(title));
5                  put course= title=;
6              run;

COURSE=C001 TITLE=Basic Telecommunications
COURSE=C002 TITLE=Structured Query Language
COURSE=C003 TITLE=Local Area Networks
COURSE=C004 TITLE=Database Design
COURSE=C005 TITLE=Artificial Intelligence
COURSE=C006 TITLE=Computer Aided Design
```

The DATA step creates the following macro variables:

Symbol Table

Variable	Value
C001	Basic Telecommunications
C002	Structured Query Language
C003	Local Area Networks
C004	Database Design
C005	Artificial Intelligence
C006	Computer Aided Design

Creating Multiple Macro Variables with SYMPUT

Example: Resolve the macro variables for specified values of COURSE.

```
data _null_;
   set perm.courses;
   call symput(course,trim(title));
run;
%let crsid=C005;
proc print data=perm.schedule noobs label;
   where course="&crsid";
   var location begin teacher;
   title1 "Schedule for &c005";
run;
%let crsid=C002;
proc print data=perm.schedule noobs label;
   where course="&crsid";
   var location begin teacher;
   title1 "Schedule for &c002";
run;
```

This solution can be improved if the value of the CRSID macro variable could also serve to reference one of the macro variables C001, C002, and so on.

```
%let crsid=C002;
proc print data=perm.schedule noobs label;
   where course="&crsid";
   var location begin teacher;
   title1 "Schedule for ?????";
run;
```

Indirect References to Macro Variables

You can use multiple ampersands in front of a macro variable name to allow the value of a macro variable to become another macro variable reference.

Rescan Rule:

- Multiple ampersands or percent signs preceding a name token cause the macro processor to rescan the reference.

- Two ampersands (&&) resolve to one ampersand (&).

Forward Scan Rule:

- To rescan a reference, the macro processor continues scanning and resolving until a token is encountered that cannot be part of the macro trigger being scanned.

- After the initial scan, a second scan begins left to right from the point where multiple ampersands or percent signs are coded.

- If a macro reference contains four or more &s, additional scans are performed from left to right until no more triggers can be resolved.

Indirect References to Macro Variables

Example: Use the value of CRSID to create a reference for another macro variable.

Symbol Table

Variable	Value
C001	Basic Telecommunications
C002	Structured Query Language
C003	Local Area Networks
C004	Database Design
C005	Artificial Intelligence
C006	Computer Aided Design
CRSID	C002

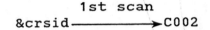

```
        1st scan
&crsid ──────────► C002
```

```
        1st scan        2nd scan
&&crsid ─────────► &crsid ─────────► C002
```

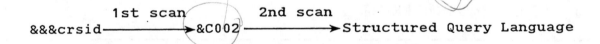

```
        1st scan        2nd scan
&&&crsid ────────► &C002 ─────────► Structured Query Language
```

Indirect References to Macro Variables

Example: Use indirect referencing to improve the last application. Assume that a
LOOKUP2 fileref is assigned to the file below.

Fileref = LOOKUP2

```
proc print data=perm.schedule noobs label;
   where course="&crsid";
   var location begin teacher;
   title1 "Schedule for &&&crsid";
run;
```
(title of course)

This program creates the desired reports.

```
libname perm 'edc.macro.sasdata' disp=shr;
filename lookup2 'edc.macro.sascode(lookup2)';
options symbolgen source2;
data _null_;
   set perm.courses;
   call symput(course,trim(title));
run;
%let crsid=C005;
%include lookup2;
%let crsid=C002;
%include lookup2;
```

Output from First PROC PRINT

```
            Schedule for Artificial Intelligence

        Location     Begin         Instructor

        Dallas       08APR91     Hallis, Dr. George
        Seattle      29JUL91     Tally, Ms. Julia
        Boston       21OCT91     Hallis, Dr. George
```

Indirect References to Macro Variables

Partial SAS Log

```
13          %let crsid=C005;
14          %include lookup2;

NOTE: %INCLUDE (level 1) file LOOKUP2 is file
      EDC.MACRO.SASCODE(LOOKUP2).
15          +proc print data=perm.schedule noobs label;
16          +   where course="&crsid";

SYMBOLGEN:  Macro variable CRSID resolves to C005
17          +   var location begin teacher;
18          +

SYMBOLGEN:  && resolves to &.
SYMBOLGEN:  Macro variable CRSID resolves to C005
SYMBOLGEN:  Macro variable C005 resolves to Artificial Intelligence
18          +   title1 "Schedule for &&&crsid";
19          +run;

NOTE: %INCLUDE (level 1) ending.
20          %let crsid=C002;
21          %include lookup2;

NOTE: %INCLUDE (level 1) file LOOKUP2 is file
      EDC.MACRO.SASCODE(LOOKUP2).
22          +proc print data=perm.schedule noobs label;
23          +   where course="&crsid";

SYMBOLGEN:  Macro variable CRSID resolves to C002
24          +   var location begin teacher;

SYMBOLGEN:  && resolves to &.
SYMBOLGEN:  Macro variable CRSID resolves to C002
SYMBOLGEN:  Macro variable C002 resolves to Structured Query Language
25          +   title1 "Schedule for &&&crsid";
26          +run;

NOTE: %INCLUDE (level 1) ending.
```

Indirect References to Macro Variables

Indirect referencing is also useful in applications where you need to create a list of related macro variables.

Example: Create a series of macro variables TEACH1 to TEACH*n*, each containing the name of the instructor assigned to a specific course. Reference one of these variables when a course number is designated.

```
options symbolgen;
data _null_;
    set perm.schedule;
    call symput('teach'||left(crsnum),trim(teacher));
run;
%let crs=3;
proc print data=perm.register noobs;
    where crsnum=&crs;
    var name paid;
    title1 "Roster for Course &crs";
    title2 "Taught by &&teach&crs";
run;
```

Symbol Table

Variable	Value
TEACH1	Hallis, Dr. George
TEACH2	Wickam, Dr. Alice
TEACH3	Forest, Mr. Peter
.	
.	
.	
CRS	3

```
          1st scan              2nd scan
&&teach&crs ───────► &teach3 ───────► Forest, Mr. Peter
```

Indirect References to Macro Variables

Partial SAS Log

```
7            %let crs=3;
8            proc print data=perm.register noobs;
9               where crsnum=&crs;

SYMBOLGEN:   Macro variable CRS resolves to 3
10              var name paid;

SYMBOLGEN:   Macro variable CRS resolves to 3
11              title1 "Roster for Course &crs";

SYMBOLGEN:   && resolves to &.
SYMBOLGEN:   Macro variable CRS resolves to 3
SYMBOLGEN:   Macro variable TEACH3 resolves to Forest, Mr. Peter
12              title2 "Taught by &&teach&crs";
13           run;
```

Partial Output

```
              Roster for Course 3
            Taught by Forest, Mr. Peter

        NAME                    PAID

        Bills, Ms. Paulette       Y
        Chevarley, Ms. Arlene     N
        Clough, Ms. Patti         N
        Crace, Mr. Ron            Y
        Davis, Mr. Bruce          Y
```

Other examples of using a series of macro variables as an array structure are presented in Chapter 5.

3.2 The SYMGET Function

Introduction

You can obtain a macro variable's value during DATA step execution using the SYMGET function.

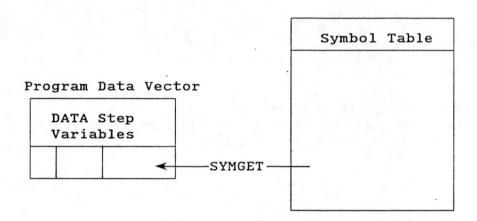

The SYMGET function returns the value of an existing macro variable.

General form of the SYMGET function:

SYMGET(*macro-variable*)

macro-variable   can be specified as a

- character literal

- DATA step character expression.

The SYMGET function truncates any macro variable value longer than 200 characters.

A DATA step variable created by the SYMGET function is a character variable with a length of 200 bytes unless it has been previously defined.

Introduction

Example: Obtain the values of the SITE and PENALTY macro variables using
SYMGET functions.

```
%let site=Seattle;
%let penalty=.06;
data overdue(drop=paid location);
    set perm.all(keep=name course location begin fee paid);
    where paid='N' and location=symget('site');
    latefee=fee*input(symget('penalty'),3.);
    newfee=fee+latefee;
    format latefee dollar8.2 newfee dollar10.2;
run;
proc print data=overdue;
    title "Unpaid Students at &site Training Center";
run;
```

(handwritten annotations: "Change to Num", "&SITE", "& PENALTY")

Partial Output

```
                 Unpaid Students at Seattle Training Center

OBS NAME                        COURSE   BEGIN     FEE   LATEFEE      NEWFEE

  1 Babbitt, Mr. Bill           C001    10JUN91   $795   $47.70     $842.70
  2 Coley, Mr. John             C001    10JUN91   $795   $47.70     $842.70
  3 Sanders, Ms. Julie          C001    10JUN91   $795   $47.70     $842.70
  4 Vandenberg, Mr. Kurt        C001    10JUN91   $795   $47.70     $842.70
  5 Kendig, Ms. Linda           C002    17JUN91  $1150   $69.00   $1,219.00
  6 Leon, Mr. Quinton           C002    17JUN91  $1150   $69.00   $1,219.00
```

Could you create the same report by using macro variable references in the DATA
step instead of SYMGET functions?

(handwritten: "YES!", "& PENALTY", "& SITE")

Introduction

Exercise: State the type, length, and value of the DATA step variables in the
program below.

```
%let var1=cat;
%let var2=3;
        VAR3 = dog;

data test;
    length s1 s4 s5 $ 3;

    call symput('var3','dog');

    r1="&var1";      "CAT"

    r2=&var2;        3

    r3="&var3";      &VAR3"

    s1=symget('var1');

    s2=symget('var2');

    s3=input(symget('var2'),2.);

    s4=symget('var3');

    s5=symget('var'||left(r2));
run;                 (VAR 3)
                      DOG
```

DOESN'T COMPILE &VAR3

Compile time | Execution time

NAME	TYPE	LENGTH	VALUE
R1	$	3	CAT
R2	N	8	3
R3	$	5	&VAR3
S1	$	3	CAT
S2	$	200	3 (199 8/VK)
S3	N	8	3
S4	$	3	DOG
S5	$	3	(VAR 3)=DOG

What type of applications would require the use of the SYMGET function instead
of simple macro variable referencing?

Compilers   Versus   Data maintaining

Applications for SYMGET

Suppose the program shown below is used frequently. Different values are supplied for the macro variables COMP and END.

```
%let comp=Special Services;
%let end=30Sep91;
data subset;
    set perm.all end=final;
    where company="&comp" and begin le "&end"d;
    if paid='Y' then pay+fee;
    else nopay+fee;
    if final then do;
        call symput('good',left(put(pay,dollar10.)));
        call symput('bad',left(put(nopay,dollar10.)));
    end;
run;
proc print data=subset;
    var name course location begin paid fee;
    title1 "Students from &comp as of &end";
    title2 "Paid Revenue Is &good";
    title3 "Unpaid Revenue Is &bad";
run;
```

```
              Students from Special Services as of 30Sep91
                      Paid Revenue Is $1,990
                     Unpaid Revenue Is $1,600

    OBS        NAME          COURSE LOCATION   BEGIN  PAID   FEE

     1   Albritton, Mr. Bryan   C001  Dallas   04FEB91  Y    $795
     2   Albritton, Mr. Bryan   C005  Dallas   08APR91  Y    $400
     3   Lawee, Mr. Jackie      C006  Dallas   06MAY91  N   $1600
     4   Lawee, Mr. Jackie      C001  Seattle  10JUN91  Y    $795
```

Applications for SYMGET

To make the program run more efficiently, you can store a compiled image of the DATA step using the Stored Program Facility.

Example: Use the PGM = *stored-program-name* option in the DATA statement to create a permanent SAS file named PERM.SUBSET1 containing the compiled DATA step statements.

```
libname perm 'edc.macro.sasdata' disp=old;
%let comp=Special Services;
%let end=30Sep91;
data subset / pgm=perm.subset1;
   set perm.all end=final;
   where company="&comp" and begin le "&end"d;
   if paid='Y' then pay+fee;
   else nopay+fee;
   if final then do;
      call symput('good',left(put(pay,dollar10.)));
      call symput('bad',left(put(nopay,dollar10.)));
   end;
run;
```

(handwritten annotation: Stored in Compiled Form)

Partial SAS Log

```
NOTE: DATA STEP program saved on file PERM.SUBSET1.
NOTE: The original source statements cannot be retrieved from a
      stored DATA STEP program nor will a stored DATA STEP
      program run under a different release of the SAS system
      or under a different operating system.
      Please be sure to save the source statements for this
      stored program.
```

Note: PERM.SUBSET1 has a member type of PROGRAM in the SAS data library.

This DATA step does not execute the stored statements. The SUBSET data set is not created.

Applications for SYMGET

To execute a stored DATA step, specify its name in a DATA statement.

Example: Execute the stored program PERM.SUBSET1.

```
data pgm=perm.subset1;
run;
```

Partial SAS Log

```
NOTE: DATA STEP program loaded from file PERM.SUBSET1.
NOTE: The data set WORK.SUBSET has 4 observations and 14
      variables.
```

Applications for SYMGET

Suppose you want to supply new values for the macro variables COMP and END using the stored program PERM.SUBSET1. Examine the listings shown on the next page.

```
%let comp=Special Services;
%let end=30Sep91;
data pgm=perm.subset1;
proc print data=subset;
    var name course location begin paid fee;
    title1 "Students from &comp as of &end";
    title2 "Paid Revenue Is &good";
    title3 "Unpaid Revenue Is &bad";
run;


%let comp=Reston Railway;
%let end=30Mar91;
data pgm=perm.subset1;
proc print data=subset;
    var name course location begin paid fee;
    title1 "Students from &comp as of &end";
    title2 "Paid Revenue Is &good";
    title3 "Unpaid Revenue Is &bad";
run;
```

Applications for SYMGET

Program Output

```
          Students from Special Services as of 30Sep91
                    Paid Revenue Is $1,990
                   Unpaid Revenue Is $1,600

  OBS          NAME          COURSE LOCATION   BEGIN PAID   FEE

   1   Albritton, Mr. Bryan  C001   Dallas    04FEB91  Y   $795
   2   Albritton, Mr. Bryan  C005   Dallas    08APR91  Y   $400
   3   Lawee, Mr. Jackie     C006   Dallas    06MAY91  N  $1600
   4   Lawee, Mr. Jackie     C001   Seattle   10JUN91  Y   $795
```

```
          Students from Reston Railway as of 30Mar91
                    Paid Revenue Is $1,990
                   Unpaid Revenue Is $1,600

  OBS          NAME          COURSE LOCATION   BEGIN PAID   FEE

   1   Albritton, Mr. Bryan  C001   Dallas    04FEB91  Y   $795
   2   Albritton, Mr. Bryan  C005   Dallas    08APR91  Y   $400
   3   Lawee, Mr. Jackie     C006   Dallas    06MAY91  N  $1600
   4   Lawee, Mr. Jackie     C001   Seattle   10JUN91  Y   $795
```

Note that the values of the macro variables COMP and END changed in the first title line as expected.

Why are both listings the same?

Applications for SYMGET

By using the SYMGET functions in the DATA step below, you avoid the premature resolution of the macro variable references.

```
data subset / pgm=perm.subset2;
   set perm.all end=final;
   where company=symget('comp') and
         begin le input(symget('end'),date7.);
   if paid='Y' then pay+fee;
   else nopay+fee;
   if final then do;
      call symput('good',left(put(pay,dollar10.)));
      call symput('bad',left(put(nopay,dollar10.)));
   end;
run;
```

The macro variables COMP and END do **not** have to exist when this program is compiled.

Applications for SYMGET

Suppose you want to supply values for the macro variables COMP and END using the stored program PERM.SUBSET2. Compare the listings on the next page with the ones generated by the PERM.SUBSET1 program.

```
%let comp=Special Services;
%let end=30Sep91;
data pgm=perm.subset2;
proc print data=subset;
   var name course location begin paid fee;
   title1 "Students from &comp as of &end";
   title2 "Paid Revenue Is &good";
   title3 "Unpaid Revenue Is &bad";
run;


%let comp=Reston Railway;
%let end=30Mar91;
data pgm=perm.subset2;
proc print data=subset;
   var name course location begin paid fee;
   title1 "Students from &comp as of &end";
   title2 "Paid Revenue Is &good";
   title3 "Unpaid Revenue Is &bad";
run;
```

First Listing

```
          Students from Special Services as of 30Sep91
                     Paid Revenue Is $1,990
                    Unpaid Revenue Is $1,600

  OBS        NAME         COURSE LOCATION   BEGIN  PAID    FEE

    1   Albritton, Mr. Bryan  C001  Dallas   04FEB91   Y     $795
    2   Albritton, Mr. Bryan  C005  Dallas   08APR91   Y     $400
    3   Lawee, Mr. Jackie     C006  Dallas   06MAY91   N    $1600
    4   Lawee, Mr. Jackie     C001  Seattle  10JUN91   Y     $795
```

Applications for SYMGET

Second Listing

```
          Students from Reston Railway as of 30Mar91
                  Paid Revenue Is $2,700
                 Unpaid Revenue Is $2,095

    OBS        NAME         COURSE  LOCATION   BEGIN   PAID   FEE

     1    Haubold, Ms. Ann    C001   Dallas   04FEB91    N    $795
     2    Bills, Ms. Paulette C003   Dallas   11MAR91    Y    $650
     3    Clough, Ms. Patti   C003   Dallas   11MAR91    N    $650
     4    Haubold, Ms. Ann    C003   Dallas   11MAR91    Y    $650
     5    Kochen, Mr. Dennis  C003   Dallas   11MAR91    Y    $650
     6    Smith, Ms. Jan      C003   Dallas   11MAR91    N    $650
     7    Bates, Ms. Ellen    C004   Dallas   25MAR91    Y    $375
     8    Swayze, Mr. Rodney  C004   Dallas   25MAR91    Y    $375
```

The SYMGET function should be used when you want to obtain the value of a macro variable during run time instead of when a source program is "compiled".

This principle also applies to

- DATA step views

- SQL views

- SCL programs.

3.3 The SQL Interface (Optional)

Introduction

Structured Query Language (SQL) coding is placed into an input stack and word scanning is performed for macro triggers in the same process as other SAS programs.

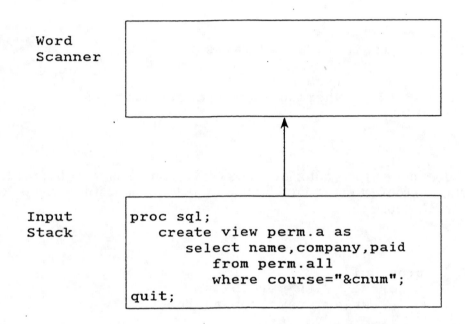

```
Word
Scanner



Input        proc sql;
Stack            create view perm.a as
                     select name,company,paid
                         from perm.all
                         where course="&cnum";
             quit;
```

As in the example of using macro variable references in a stored DATA step program, the macro variable reference &CNUM is resolved during the creation of the SQL view, resulting in a constant value whenever the view is used.

Introduction

SQL supports the SYMGET function. This allows views to look up macro variable values when views are used.

The rules regarding the use of literals or expressions for its argument are exactly the same as the DATA step.

The example below illustrates coding when making comparisons to a character variable COURSE.

```
proc sql;
    create view perm.a as
        select name,company,paid
            from perm.all
            where course=symget('cnum');
quit;
```

SQL does not perform automatic data conversion. You must use the INPUT function to convert the macro variable value to numeric if it is compared to a numeric variable.

```
proc sql;
    create view perm.b as
        select name,company,paid
            from perm.all
            where crsnum=input(symget('num'),2.);
quit;
```

The INTO Clause

The SQL procedure does not have a SYMPUT routine.

Instead, you use the INTO clause in a SELECT statement to specify one or more macro variables to create (update).

General form of the INTO clause:

> **SELECT** *col1, col2, . . .* **INTO:***mvar1,:mvar2, . . .*
>   FROM *table-expression*
>   WHERE *where-expression*
>   *other clauses* ;

Example: Create a macro variable named TOTFEE that contains the total of all course fees. Use this macro variable in a later step.

```
proc sql noprint;
   select sum(fee) format=dollar10. into:totfee
       from perm.all;
%let totfee=&totfee;
proc means data=perm.all sum maxdec=0;
   class title;
   var fee;
   title "Grand Total for All Courses Is &totfee";
run;
```

Note: If a SELECT statement produces more than one row of output, any macro variables specified in the INTO clause receive values from the first row.

The INTO clause stores the formatted value of SUM(FEE) in the macro variable TOTFEE, including any leading or trailing blanks.

The %LET statement removes any leading or trailing blanks that might be stored in the value of TOTFEE.

The INTO Clause

Program Output

```
            Grand Total for All Courses Is $354,380

    Analysis Variable : FEE Course Fee


    TITLE                              N Obs          Sum
    ---------------------------------------------------------
    Artificial Intelligence             71          28400

    Basic Telecommunications            69          54855

    Computer Aided Design               66         105600

    Database Design                     77          28875

    Local Area Networks                 74          48100

    Structured Query Language           77          88550
    ---------------------------------------------------------
```

The INTO Clause

Some applications require multiple passes of the data to compute desired statistics.

Example: Use PROC MEANS, PROC SORT, and the DATA step to create a
macro variable named COMP that contains the name of the company
that sent the most students to courses during a specified time period.
Create the macro variable MAX to contain the number of students sent
by this company.

```
%let start=1Jan91;
%let stop=31Dec91;
proc means data=perm.all(keep=company begin) noprint;
   where begin between "&start"d and "&stop"d;
   class company;
   var begin;
   output out=counts n=freq;
run;
proc sort data=counts;
   by descending freq;
   where _type_=1;
run;
data _null_;
   set counts;
   call symput('max',left(freq));
   call symput('comp',trim(company));
   stop;
run;
proc print data=perm.all noobs;
   where begin between "&start"d and "&stop"d and
         company="&comp";
   var name course location begin;
   title1 "&comp Sent the Most Students (&max)";
   title2 "Between &start and &stop";
run;
```

The INTO Clause

You may find the SQL coding for computing the macro variable values simpler.

```
%let start=1Jan91;
%let stop=31Dec91;
proc sql noprint;
    select company,num into :comp,:max
        from (select company,n(company) as num
                from perm.all
                where begin between "&start"d and "&stop"d
                group by company)
        having num=max(num);
%let comp=&comp;
%let max=&max;
proc print data=perm.all noobs;
    where begin between "&start"d and "&stop"d and
            company="&comp";
    var name course location begin;
    options nodate nonumber;
    title1 "&comp Sent the Most Students (&max)";
    title2 "Between &start and &stop";
run;
```

The INTO Clause

Output from Either Program

```
              Reston Railway Sent the Most Students (30)
                    Between 1Jan91 and 31Dec91

              NAME              COURSE    LOCATION      BEGIN

       Haubold, Ms. Ann          C001     Dallas       04FEB91
       Bills, Ms. Paulette       C003     Dallas       11MAR91
       Clough, Ms. Patti         C003     Dallas       11MAR91
       Haubold, Ms. Ann          C003     Dallas       11MAR91
       Kochen, Mr. Dennis        C003     Dallas       11MAR91
       Smith, Ms. Jan            C003     Dallas       11MAR91
       Bates, Ms. Ellen          C004     Dallas       25MAR91
       Swayze, Mr. Rodney        C004     Dallas       25MAR91
       Kochen, Mr. Dennis        C006     Dallas       06MAY91
       Smith, Mr. Jack           C006     Dallas       06MAY91
       Avakian, Mr. Don          C001     Seattle      10JUN91
       Bates, Ms. Ellen          C001     Seattle      10JUN91
       Truell, Ms. Joleen        C001     Seattle      10JUN91
       Garrett, Mr. Tom          C003     Seattle      08JUL91
       Howell, Mr. Jody          C003     Seattle      08JUL91
       Bills, Ms. Paulette       C005     Seattle      29JUL91
       Swayze, Mr. Rodney        C005     Seattle      29JUL91
       Truell, Ms. Joleen        C005     Seattle      29JUL91
       Swayze, Mr. Rodney        C001     Boston       09SEP91
       Alamutu, Ms. Julie        C002     Boston       16SEP91
       Avakian, Mr. Don          C002     Boston       16SEP91
       Garrett, Mr. Tom          C002     Boston       16SEP91
       Swayze, Mr. Rodney        C002     Boston       16SEP91
       Wallace, Mr. Jules        C003     Boston       23SEP91
       Clough, Ms. Patti         C004     Boston       07OCT91
       Garrett, Mr. Tom          C004     Boston       07OCT91
       Truell, Ms. Joleen        C004     Boston       07OCT91
       Haubold, Ms. Ann          C005     Boston       21OCT91
       Smith, Mr. Jack           C005     Boston       21OCT91
       Bates, Ms. Ellen          C006     Boston       11NOV91
```

3.4 The SCL Interface (Optional)

Introduction

SAS/AF, SAS/FSP, and SAS/CALC software support Screen Control Language (SCL) programs.

SCL programs are placed into an input stack and word scanning is performed for macro triggers in the same process as other SAS programs.

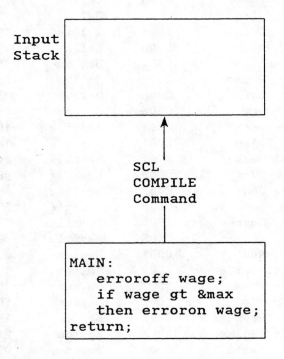

In the above example, the stored value of the macro variable MAX is resolved during SCL **compilation.** Its value cannot change during SCL execution.

You must recompile the program to reset the value of MAX.

Introduction

SCL offers two routines and two functions to interface with the macro facility during SCL **execution.**

CALL SYMPUT(*macro-variable,character value*);

CALL SYMPUTN(*macro-variable,numeric value*);

cval = **SYMGET**(*macro-variable*);

nval = **SYMGETN**(*macro-variable*);

Rules regarding the use of literals or expressions for arguments are exactly the same as the DATA step.

The SYMPUTN routine expects a numeric second argument. The routine stores a trimmed left-aligned character equivalent (using BEST12. format) of this argument.

The SYMGETN function returns the numeric equivalent of the macro variable's value.

A Simple Example

One of the most common applications for these routines and functions is to pass information between PROGRAM entries.

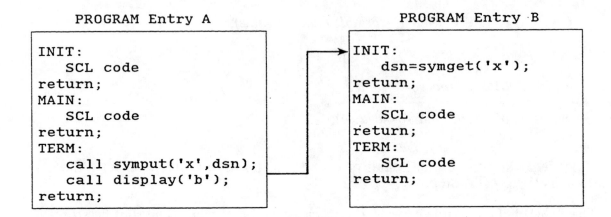

In this diagram,

- global macro variable X is given the value of the SCL variable DSN as the user leaves PROGRAM entry A

- control is passed to PROGRAM entry B

- SCL variable DSN in PROGRAM entry B is initialized with the value of the macro variable X.

3.5 Exercises

3.1   Creating Macro Variables with the SYMPUT Routine

    a.   Reset the system option DATE|NODATE to NODATE. Write a DATA step that creates a macro variable named DATE. This variable's value should be today's date in the MMDDYY8. format. (Hint: Use a PUT function to format the result of the TODAY function.) Verify that DATE has the proper value by submitting the following TITLE statement:

```
title "Courses Offered as of &date";
```

          and then printing the PERM.COURSES data set.

    b.   Recall the DATA step and modify it so that DATE has a value that uses the WORDDATE20. format (*month dd, year*). Print the PERM.COURSES data set again. (Make sure there are not any extra blanks in the title.)

3.2   Creating Macro Variables with the SYMPUT Routine

    a.   Submit a **%LET** statement to create a macro variable named STATE with the value **MD** .

    b.   Use a DATA step to create a temporary data set named STUDENTS containing a subset of the PERM.STUDENTS data set:

- Include only those students from the state specified by the STATE macro variable.
- Create a new DATA step variable CITY from the CITYST variable that has only the city name for its values.
- Create a macro variable named STNAME from the STATE macro variable that has the full state name as its value. Use the STNAMEL function to convert a postal code to the state name. For example, **STNAMEL('OH')** returns **Ohio** .
- Drop CITYST from the output data set.

Exercises

3.2   Creating Macro Variables with the SYMPUT Routine (continued)

c.   Print the STUDENTS data set with a title that includes a reference to the STNAME macro variable.

d.   Change the value of the STATE macro variable to FL. Resubmit the DATA step and print STUDENTS again. Verify the listing.

3.3   Resolving Macro Variables with the SYMGET Routine

a.   Modify the DATA step from Exercise 3.2 so that references to the STATE macro variable are resolved during DATA step execution. Test your coding by changing the value of STATE to MI and printing the STUDENTS data set.

b.   Recall the DATA step and create a stored program named STUDENTS from it.

c.   Change the value of STATE to CA, execute the stored program, and print the STUDENTS data set. Change the value of STATE to TX, execute the stored program, and print the STUDENTS data set.

Exercises

page 106

3.4   Creating Multiple Macro Variables

a.   The PERM.SCHEDULE data set contains the variable BEGIN, which contains the beginning date of each course. Use a DATA step to create a series of macro variables named START1 through START*n*, one for each course offered. The value of each START variable should be the date in the MMDDYY8. format.

b.   Include the program C3EX4 shown below. Modify the TITLE statement so the series of Xs is replaced with an indirect macro variable reference to one of the START variables based on the current value of CRS.

```
%let crs=4;
proc print data=perm.all noobs n;
   where crsnum=&crs;
   var name company;
   title "Roster for Course &crs Beginning on XXXXXX";
run;
```

c.   Change the value of CRS to 15. Resubmit the PROC PRINT step. Verify that a different START variable has been referenced.

3.5   Creating Macro Variables Using the SYMPUT Routine (Optional)

a.   Use the DATA step to create one macro variable named SITES that contains the names of all training centers that appear in the PERM.SCHEDULE data set. The names should be separated by one blank. (Hint: Use PROC FREQ to create a data set with one observation per value of LOCATION. Read this data set and concatenate the LOCATION values before executing the SYMPUT routine.)

b.   Generate a report with PROC MEANS that displays the total revenue from all students in PERM.ALL (use the FEE variable). Include a TITLE statement that references the SITES macro variable.

3.6 Chapter Summary

Normally, all macro processing takes place prior to the execution of a SAS step. The DATA step and PROC SQL enable you to create and resolve macro variables during step execution. This is important when you want to assign values of SAS variables to macro variables or have SAS variables take on macro variable values during step execution.

The SYMPUT routine in the DATA step creates or updates variables. Depending on how the arguments are coded, you can create a single macro variable or multiple macro variables.

The INTO clause in the SELECT statement performs a similar operation for the SQL procedure.

The SYMGET function is used by both the DATA step and SQL procedure to import the value of a macro variable.

It is possible to construct macro variable references that contain two or more ampersands. This technique is useful when you want to use a macro variable to construct the name of another macro variable.

General form of the SYMPUT routine:

CALL SYMPUT(*macro-variable,text*);

General form of the SYMPUT routine with literals:

CALL SYMPUT(*'macro-variable','text'*);

General form of the SYMPUT routine with a literal and variable:

CALL SYMPUT(*'macro-variable',DATA-step-variable*);

Chapter Summary

General form of the SYMPUT routine with a DATA step expression:

CALL SYMPUT(*'macro-variable'*,*expression*);

General form of the SYMPUT routine to create multiple macro variables:

CALL SYMPUT(*expression1*,*expression2*);

General form of the SYMGET function:

SYMGET(*macro-variable*)

General form of the INTO clause:

SELECT *col1, col2, . . .* **INTO:***mvar1,:mvar2, . . .*
    FROM *table-expression*
    WHERE *where-expression*
    other clauses ;

General form of the SYMPUT and SYMPUTN routines used in SCL:

CALL SYMPUT(*macro-variable,character value*);

CALL SYMPUTN(*macro-variable,numeric value*);

General form of the SYMGET and SYMGETN functions used in SCL:

cval = **SYMGET**(*macro-variable*);

nval = **SYMGETN**(*macro-variable*);

3.7 Solutions and Selected Output

3.1   **Creating Macro Variables with the SYMPUT Routine**

a.

```
options nodate;
data _null_;
   call symput('date',put(today(),
        mmddyy8.));
run;
title "Courses offered as of &date";
```

b.

```
data _null_;
   call symput('date',left(put(today(),
        worddate20.)));
run;
title "Courses offered as of &date";
```

3.2   **Creating Macro Variables with the SYMPUT Routine**

a.

```
%let state=MD;
```

b.

```
data students(drop=cityst);
   set perm.students end=last;
   where cityst contains "&state";
   city=scan(cityst,1,',');
   if last then
      call symput('stname',
           trim(stnamel("&state")));
run;
```

Solutions and Selected Output

3.2   Creating Macro Variables with the SYMPUT Routine (continued)

c.

```
proc print data=students;
    title "Students from &stname";
run;
```

```
                      Students from Maryland

OBS          NAME              COMPANY                    CITY

 1    Allen, Ms. Denise     Department of Defense    Bethesda
 2    Brown, Mr. Michael    Swain Diagnostics Inc.   Columbia
 3    Elsins, Ms. Marisa F. SSS Inc.                 Annapolis
 4    Shew, Ms. Marguerite  SSS Inc.                 Annapolis
```

d.

```
%let state=FL;
```

```
                      Students from Florida

OBS          NAME              COMPANY              CITY

 1    Chavez, Ms. Louise      US Express Corp.   Fort Lauderdale
 2    Dellmonache, Ms. Susan  US Express Corp.   Fort Lauderdale
 3    Schwoebel, Mr. Roger    WAVCOMP            Pensacola
 4    Ziegler, Mr. David      US Express Corp.   Fort Lauderdale
```

Solutions and Selected Output

3.3   Resolving Macro Variables with the SYMGET Routine

a.

```
%let state=MI;
data students(drop=cityst);
   set perm.students end=last;
   where cityst contains symget('state');
   city=scan(cityst,1,',');
   if last then
      call symput('stname',
          trim(stnamel(symget('state'))));
run;
proc print data=students;
   title "Students from &stname";
run;
```

```
                 Students from Michigan

OBS        NAME              COMPANY                        CITY

 1    Holbrook, Ms. Amy    Wooster Chemical                Midland
 2    McLaughlin, Ms. Amy  Wooster Chemical                Midland
 3    Pancoast, Ms. Jane   Chase Information Technology    Detroit
 4    Peterson, Ms. Julie  Chase Information Technology    Detroit
```

b.

```
data students(drop=cityst) / pgm=students;
   set perm.students end=last;
   where cityst contains symget('state');
   city=scan(cityst,1,',');
   if last then
      call symput('stname',
          trim(stnamel(symget('state'))));
run;
```

Solutions and Selected Output

3.3   Resolving Macro Variables with the SYMGET Routine (continued)

c.

```
%let state=CA;
data pgm=students;
proc print data=students;
    title "Students from &stname";
run;

%let state=TX;
data pgm=students;
proc print data=students;
    title "Students from &stname";
run;
```

There are 62 students from California.

There are 5 students from Texas.

3.4   Creating Multiple Macro Variables

a.

```
data _null_;
    set perm.schedule;
    call symput('start'||trim(left(_n_)),
        put(begin,mmddyy8.));
run;
```

Solutions and Selected Output

3.4   Creating Multiple Macro Variables (continued)

b.

```
%let crs=4;
proc print data=perm.all noobs n;
    where crsnum=&crs;
    var name company;
    title "Roster for Course &crs "
          "Beginning on &&start&crs";
run;
```

Partial Output

```
            Roster for Course 4 Beginning on 03/25/91

NAME                        COMPANY

Bates, Ms. Ellen            Reston Railway
Boyd, Ms. Leah              United Shoes Co.
Chan, Mr. John              California Lawyers Assn.
Chevarley, Ms. Arlene       Motor Communications
Chow, Ms. Sylvia            Bostic Amplifier Inc.
Crace, Mr. Ron              Von Crump Seafood
```

Solutions and Selected Output

3.4   **Creating Multiple Macro Variables** (continued)

c.

```
%let crs=15;
proc print data=perm.all noobs n;
    where crsnum=&crs;
    var name company;
    title "Roster for Course &crs "
          "Beginning on &&start&crs";
run;
```

Partial Output

```
                Roster for Course 15 Beginning on 09/23/91

    NAME                         COMPANY

    Chavez, Ms. Louise           US Express Corp.
    Edwards, Ms. Kathy           Allied Wood Corporation
    Garza, Ms. Cheryl            Admiral Research & Development Co.
    Gemelos, Mr. Jerry           Atlantic Airways, Inc.
    Green, Mr. Pat               K&P Products
    Hipps, Mr. Rich              Assoc. of Realtors
    Kiraly, Mr. Bill             Washington International Corp.
    Knight, Ms. Susan            K&P Products
```

Solutions and Selected Output

3.5   Creating Macro Variables Using the SYMPUT Routine (Optional)

```
proc freq data=perm.schedule noprint;
    tables location / out=temp;
data _null_;
    set temp end=last;
    length allsites $ 200;
    retain allsites;
    allsites=trim(allsites)||' '||location;
    if last then call symput('sites',
        trim(left(allsites)));
run;
```

b.

```
proc means data=perm.all sum maxdec=0;
    var fee;
    title "Total Revenue from Course Sites: &sites";
run;
```

```
Total Revenue from Course Sites: Boston Dallas Seattle

              Analysis Variable : FEE Course Fee


                         Sum
                     ------------
                        354380
                     ------------
```

4. Defining and Executing Macros

4.1 Introduction

The Need for Macro-Level Programming

Suppose you submit the following program every day to create registration listings for courses to be held during the current month.

Filename=EDC.MACRO.SASCODE(DAILY)

```
libname perm 'edc.macro.sasdata' disp=shr;
proc sort data=perm.all out=current;
   where month(begin)=month("&sysdate"d) and
         day(begin) ge day("&sysdate"d);
   by begin location title;
proc print data=current noobs n;
   var name company paid;
   by begin location title;
   title "Course Registration as of &sysdate";
run;
```

Every Friday you also submit the following program to create a summary.

Filename=EDC.MACRO.SASCODE(WEEKLY)

```
libname perm 'edc.macro.sasdata' disp=shr;
proc sort data=perm.all out=current;
   where month(begin)=month("&sysdate"d) and
         day(begin+days) le day("&sysdate"d);
   by begin location title;
proc means data=current maxdec=0 sum;
   class paid;
   var fee;
   by begin location title;
   title "Revenue for Courses as of &sysdate";
run;
```

You want to automate the process so only one program is required. This program should always submit the code in DAILY and conditionally submit the WEEKLY code.

144   Chapter 4

The Need for Macro-Level Programming

The macro facility supports programming that enables you to dynamically **write** or **edit** the code that is submitted to the SAS compiler.

Macro variables are used mainly for dynamic text substitution.

Macro programs are used to

- conditionally execute code

- repetitively execute code.

The program shown below defines a SAS *macro* that unconditionally submits code for one report and submits code for a second report if the current day is Friday.

```
%macro reports;
   %include 'edc.macro.sascode(daily)';
   %if &sysday=Friday %then %do;
       options pageno=1;
       %include 'edc.macro.sascode(weekly)';
   %end;
%mend;
```

Coding beginning with **%** signs is evaluated by the macro processor.

Note: The %INCLUDE statement is an exception. It is a global SAS statement independent of the macro facility.

You could have placed the code for both reports in the macro definition. Use the **%INCLUDE** statement to simplify programming when SAS programs already exist in external files.

The Need for Macro-Level Programming

After you have submitted the macro definition, you execute it by submitting a
macro call:

```
%reports
```

SAS Log

```
1            %macro reports;
2               %include 'edc.macro.sascode(daily)';
3               %if &sysday=Friday %then %do;
4                  options pageno=1;
5                  %include 'edc.macro.sascode(weekly)';
6               %end;
7            %mend;
8            %reports  — Submits the MACRO ABOVE
NOTE: The data set WORK.CURRENT has 24 observations and 12 variables.
NOTE: The PROCEDURE PRINT printed page 1.
```

4.2 Basic Concepts

Defining a Macro

A *macro* or *macro definition* minimally consists of a **%MACRO** statement and a **%MEND** statement.

General form of a simple macro definition:

> **%MACRO** *macro-name*;
>
> *macro-text*   (Any thing)
>
> **%MEND** *macro-name*;

The **%MACRO** statement

- begins the macro definition

- assigns a name to the macro. The value of *macro-name* is any valid SAS name that is not a **reserved word** in the macro facility.

macro-text can be

- any text

- SAS statements or steps

- macro variables, functions, or statements

- any combination of the above.

The **%MEND** statement is used to end the macro definition. Repeating *macro-name* in the **%MEND** statement is optional.

Defining a Macro

The macro facility has reserved words that cannot be used as macro names:

ABEND	ABORT	ACT	ACTIVATE	BQOUTE	BY
CLEAR	CLOSE	CMS	COMANDR	COPY	DEACT
DEL	DELETE	DISPLAY	DMIDSPLY	DMISPLIT	DO
EDIT	ELSE	END	EVAL	FILE	GLOBAL
GO	GOTO	IF	INC	INCLUDE	INDEX
INFILE	INPUT	LENGTH	LET	LIST	LISTM
LOCAL	MACRO	MEND	METASYM	NRBQUOTE	NRQUOTE
NRSTR	ON	OPEN	PAUSE	PUT	QSCAN
QSUBSTR	QUOTE	QUPCASE	RESOLVE	RETURN	RUN
SAVE	SCAN	STOP	STR	SUBSTR	SUPERQ
SYSTEM	THEN	TO	TSO	UNQUOTE	UNSTR
UNTIL	UPCASE	WHILE	WINDOW		

Example: Attempt to define a macro named LET.

SAS Log

```
1          %macro let;
ERROR: Macro LET has been given a reserved name.
ERROR: A dummy macro will be compiled.
2          %include 'edc.macro.sascode(daily)';
3          %if &sysday=Friday %then %do;
4              options pageno=1;
5              %include 'edc.macro.sascode(weekly)';
6          %end;
7          %mend;
```

What ambiguity would result if you could define a macro named LET?

%LET = Can't use

Calling a Macro

Submitting a macro definition compiles the macro.

If the macro compiles successfully, you execute it with a macro call:

%macro-name

A *macro call* (or macro reference)

- is specified by placing a percent sign before the name of the macro

- is **not** a SAS statement (does not require a semicolon)

- can be made anywhere in a program (similar to a macro variable reference).

Calling a Macro

Example: Define a simple macro that produces code to print the first five
observations from the most recently created SAS data set.

```
%macro printit;
   proc print data=_last_(obs=5);
   title 'Last Created Data Set';
   run;
%mend printit;
```

Points to the recently created data set

Suppose a program consists of several program steps that create SAS data sets.

If PRINTIT is compiled, you can reference it after each step:

```
step1
%printit
step2
%printit
step3
%printit
```

Note: An application that uses a macro for simple substitution of SAS statements
is coded more efficiently by storing the statements in

- a macro variable

- an external file and using the **%INCLUDE** statement.

Conditional Execution

You can perform conditional execution at the macro level with **%IF-%THEN** and **%ELSE** statements.

General form of **%IF-%THEN** and **%ELSE** statements:

> **%IF** *expression* **%THEN** *text*;
>
> **%ELSE** *text*;

expression   can be any valid macro expression.

The **%ELSE** statement is optional.

The *text* following the **%THEN** and **%ELSE** keywords can be

- a macro programming statement

- constant text

- an expression

- a macro variable reference

- a macro call.

Use **%DO** and **%END** statements following **%THEN** or **%ELSE** to submit text that contains semicolons.

```
%IF expression %THEN %DO;
     statement; statement; . . .
%END;

%ELSE %DO;
     statement; statement; . . .
%END;
```

Note: The macro statements on this page can **only** be used inside a macro definition.

Macro Compilation

When a macro definition is submitted, it is *compiled*.

During compilation,

- the **%MACRO** statement defines the macro name

- a SAS catalog is opened to hold the compiled macro (WORK.SASMACR by default)

- a catalog entry is created (*macro-name*.MACRO)

- macro statements are checked for syntax errors (<u>nonmacro statements are not checked</u>)   *% checking*

- all compiled macro statements and constant text are stored in the catalog entry

- the **%MEND** statement closes the entry and the catalog.

Constant text includes

- macro variable references   — *when Execution takes place*

- macro calls

- macro functions

- arithmetic and logical macro expressions

- SAS statements.

Note: If a macro definition contains macro statement syntax errors, error messages are written to the SAS log. Syntax errors create a nonexecutable (*dummy*) macro.

You can store a compiled macro in a permanent SAS catalog. This is discussed in Chapter 6.

Macro Compilation

Example: Improve the PRINTIT macro so the PROC PRINT step is submitted only if a data set is created. Introduce a syntax error and show resulting compilation messages.

```
%macro printit;
   %if &syslast ne _NULL_ % then %do;
      proc print data=_last_(obs=5);
      title "Last Created Data Set Is &syslast";
      run;
   %end;
%mend;
```

missing

SAS Log

```
1            %macro printit;
2              %if &syslast ne _NULL_   then %do;
ERROR: Macro keyword DO appears as text.  A semicolon or other
       delimiter may be missing.
ERROR: Expected %THEN statement not found.  A dummy macro will
       be compiled.
3                proc print data=_last_(obs=5);
4                title "Last Created Data Set Is &syslast";
5                run;
6            %end;
ERROR: There is no matching %DO statement for the %END. This
       statement will be ignored.
7            %mend;
```

Note: The automatic macro variable SYSLAST has the value **_NULL_** at SAS invocation.

Macro Execution

When the macro processor receives %*macro-name*, it

- searches the designated SAS catalog (WORK.SASMACR by default) for an entry named *macro-name*.MACRO

- executes compiled macro language statements

- sends any remaining text to the input stack for word scanning

- pauses execution when the SAS compiler receives a global SAS statement or a SAS step boundary

- resumes execution of macro language statements after the SAS code executes.

Macro Execution

Example: Assume the PRINTIT macro is compiled. Show processing resulting from a call to it.

```
%macro printit;
    %if &syslast ne _NULL_ %then %do;
        proc print data=_last_(obs=5);
        title "Last Created Data Set Is &syslast";
        run;
    %end;
%mend printit;


            compile


    WORK.SASMACR.PRINTIT.MACRO
```

```
%macro printit;
    %if &syslast ne _NULL_ %then %do;
        proc print data=_last_(obs=5);
        title "Last Created Data Set Is &syslast";
        run;
    %end;
%mend printit;
```

Macro Execution

When **%printit** is submitted, the macro processor locates
WORK.SASMACR.PRINTIT.MACRO.

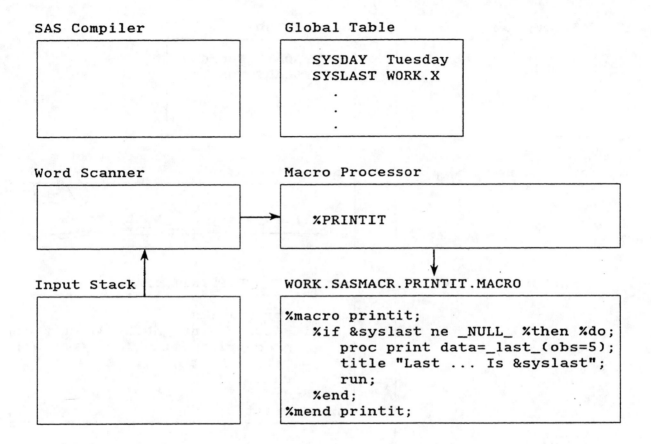

SAS Compiler

Global Table

```
SYSDAY   Tuesday
SYSLAST  WORK.X
     .
     .
     .
```

Word Scanner

Macro Processor

```
%PRINTIT
```

Input Stack

WORK.SASMACR.PRINTIT.MACRO

```
%macro printit;
   %if &syslast ne _NULL_ %then %do;
      proc print data=_last_(obs=5);
      title "Last ... Is &syslast";
      run;
   %end;
%mend printit;
```

Macro Execution

The macro processor reads the compiled code and first evaluates the **%IF**
expression. Because it is true, the **%THEN %DO** block will be processed.

SAS Compiler

```
```

Global Table

```
SYSDAY   Tuesday
SYSLAST  WORK.X
         .
         .
         .
```

Word Scanner

```
```

Macro Processor

```
%if &syslast ne _NULL_ %then ...
```

①   T or F

Input Stack

```
```

WORK.SASMACR.PRINTIT.MACRO

```
%macro printit;
   %if &syslast ne _NULL_ %then %do;
      proc print data=_last_(obs=5);
      title "Last ... Is &syslast";
      run;
   %end;
%mend printit;
```

Macro Execution

The macro processor places the text after the **%DO** on the input stack.

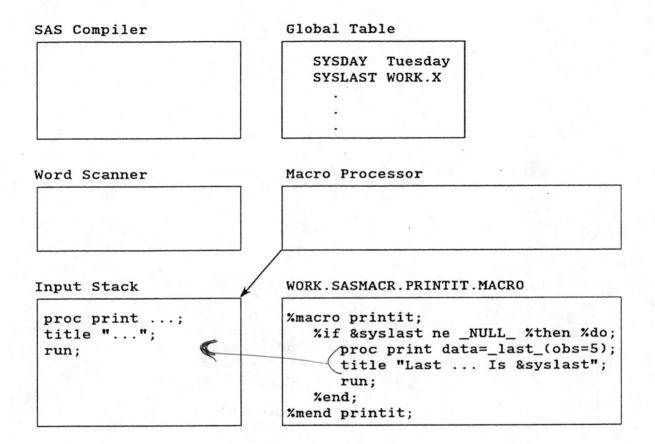

SAS Compiler

Global Table

```
SYSDAY   Tuesday
SYSLAST  WORK.X
          .
          .
          .
```

Word Scanner

Macro Processor

Input Stack

```
proc print ...;
title "...";
run;
```

WORK.SASMACR.PRINTIT.MACRO

```
%macro printit;
   %if &syslast ne _NULL_ %then %do;
      proc print data=_last_(obs=5);
      title "Last ... Is &syslast";
      run;
   %end;
%mend printit;
```

Macro Execution

Word scanning proceeds as usual.

SAS Compiler

```
PROC PRINT ...;
TITLE "...
```

Global Table

```
   SYSDAY   Tuesday
   SYSLAST  WORK.X
      .
      .
      .
```

Word Scanner

```
&SYSLAST
```

Macro Processor

```

```

Input Stack

```
             ";
run;
```

WORK.SASMACR.PRINTIT.MACRO

```
%macro printit;
   %if &syslast ne _NULL_ %then %do;
      proc print data=_last_(obs=5);
      title "Last ... Is &syslast";
      run;
   %end;
%mend printit;
```

Macro Execution

If a macro trigger is encountered, the macro reference is passed to the macro processor for resolution.

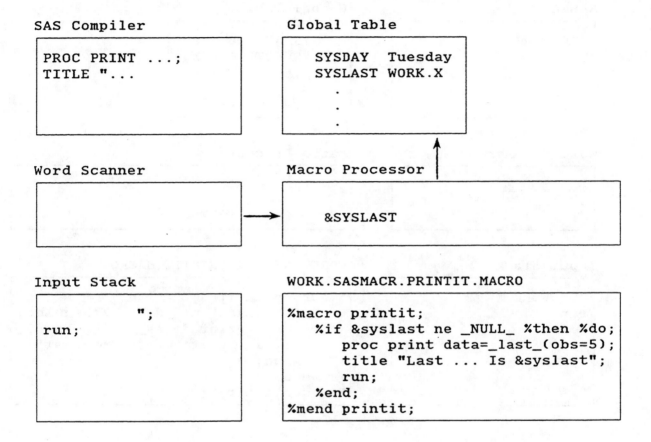

```
SAS Compiler

PROC PRINT ...;
TITLE "...
```

```
Global Table

   SYSDAY   Tuesday
   SYSLAST  WORK.X
        .
        .
        .
```

```
Word Scanner
```

```
Macro Processor

     &SYSLAST
```

```
Input Stack

            ";
 run;
```

```
WORK.SASMACR.PRINTIT.MACRO

%macro printit;
    %if &syslast ne _NULL_ %then %do;
        proc print data=_last_(obs=5);
        title "Last ... Is &syslast";
        run;
    %end;
%mend printit;
```

Macro Execution

The macro processor returns resolved values to the input stack.

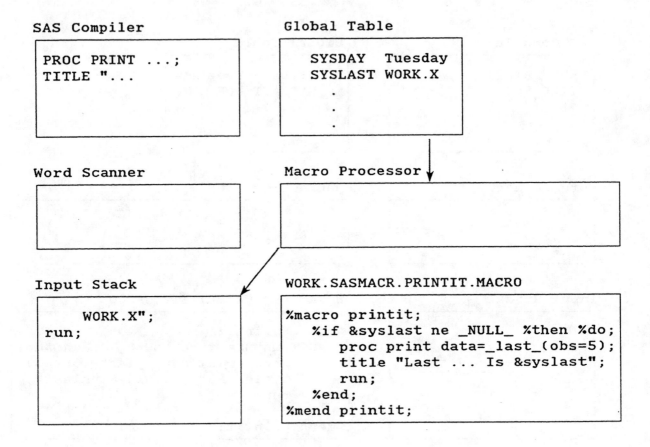

SAS Compiler

```
PROC PRINT ...;
TITLE "...
```

Global Table

```
SYSDAY   Tuesday
SYSLAST  WORK.X
         .
         .
         .
```

Word Scanner

Macro Processor

Input Stack

```
    WORK.X";
run;
```

WORK.SASMACR.PRINTIT.MACRO

```
%macro printit;
   %if &syslast ne _NULL_ %then %do;
      proc print data=_last_(obs=5);
      title "Last ... Is &syslast";
      run;
   %end;
%mend printit;
```

Macro Execution

Macro execution pauses while the PROC PRINT step executes.

SAS Compiler

```
PROC PRINT ...;
TITLE "...WORK.X";
```

Global Table

```
SYSDAY    Tuesday
SYSLAST   WORK.X
     .
     .
     .
```

Word Scanner

```
RUN;
```

Macro Processor

Input Stack

WORK.SASMACR.PRINTIT.MACRO

```
%macro printit;
   %if &syslast ne _NULL_ %then %do;
      proc print data=_last_(obs=5);
      title "Last ... Is &syslast";
      run;
   %end;
%mend printit;
```

Macro Execution

Macro execution stops when the **%MEND** statement is encountered.

```
SAS Compiler
┌─────────────────────────┐
│                         │
│                         │
│                         │
│                         │
│                         │
└─────────────────────────┘
```

```
Global Table
┌─────────────────────────┐
│  SYSDAY   Tuesday       │
│  SYSLAST  WORK.X        │
│          .              │
│          .              │
│          .              │
└─────────────────────────┘
```

```
Word Scanner
┌─────────────────────────┐
│                         │
│                         │
│                         │
│                         │
└─────────────────────────┘
```

```
Macro Processor
┌───────────────────────────────────┐
│                                   │
│                                   │
│                                   │
│                                   │
└───────────────────────────────────┘
```

```
Input Stack
┌─────────────────────────┐
│                         │
│                         │
│                         │
│                         │
│                         │
│                         │
└─────────────────────────┘
```

WORK.SASMACR.PRINTIT.MACRO

```
%macro printit;
   %if &syslast ne _NULL_ %then %do;
      proc print data=_last_(obs=5);
      title "Last ... Is &syslast";
      run;
   %end;
%mend printit;
```

Monitoring Execution

For debugging or confirmation, you might want information on an executing macro.

There are system options that instruct the macro processor to display execution information in the SAS log.

Two of the system options are

MPRINT   prints the text sent to the SAS compiler as a result of macro execution.

MLOGIC   prints messages indicating macro actions taken during macro execution.

You can specify either of these system options

- in an OPTIONS statement

- in the OPTIONS window

- at SAS invocation.

Note: The default settings of these system options are NOMPRINT and NOMLOGIC.

The MPRINT System Option

You may want to specify the MPRINT system option if you

- have a SAS syntax or execution error

- want to see the generated SAS code.

Example: Call the PRINTIT macro and show the SAS code resulting from macro execution using the MPRINT system option.

SAS Log

```
1          %macro printit;
2             %if &syslast ne _NULL_ %then %do;
3                proc print data=_last_(obs=5);
4                title "Last Created Data Set Is &syslast";
5                run;
6             %end;
7          %mend printit;
8
9          options mprint;
10         data x;
11             y=1;
12         run;

NOTE: The data set WORK.X has 1 observations and 1 variables.


13         %printit
MPRINT(PRINTIT):    PROC PRINT DATA=_LAST_(OBS=5);
MPRINT(PRINTIT):    TITLE "Last Created Data Set Is WORK.X        ";
MPRINT(PRINTIT):    RUN;

NOTE: The PROCEDURE PRINT printed page 1.
```

Note: The macro variable reference is resolved.

The MLOGIC System Option

When the MLOGIC system option is in effect, SAS log messages show

- initialization information

- the logical result of each %IF expression (true or false)

- results of other arithmetic and logical macro operations

- termination information.

Example: Repeat the previous example with only the MLOGIC system option in effect.

SAS Log

```
1          %macro printit;
2             %if &syslast ne _NULL_ %then %do;
3                proc print data=_last_(obs=5);
4                title "Last Created Data Set Is &syslast";
5                run;
6             %end;
7          %mend printit;
8
9          options mlogic;
10         data x;
11            y=1;
12         run;

NOTE: The data set WORK.X has 1 observations and 1 variables.

MLOGIC(PRINTIT):  Beginning execution.
MLOGIC(PRINTIT):  %IF condition &syslast ne _NULL_ is TRUE

13         %printit

NOTE: The PROCEDURE PRINT printed page 1.

MLOGIC(PRINTIT):  Ending execution.
```

The SYMBOLGEN System Option

Example: To obtain the values of macro variables used in logical operations, you can also specify the SYMBOLGEN system option.

SAS Log

```
1          %macro printit;
2             %if &syslast ne _NULL_ %then %do;
3                proc print data=_last_(obs=5);
4                title "Last Created Data Set Is &syslast";
5                run;
6             %end;
7          %mend printit;
8
9          options mlogic symbolgen;
10         data x;
11            y=1;
12         run;

NOTE: The data set WORK.X has 1 observations and 1 variables.

MLOGIC(PRINTIT):  Beginning execution.
SYMBOLGEN:  Macro variable SYSLAST resolves to WORK.X
MLOGIC(PRINTIT):  %IF condition &syslast ne _NULL_ is TRUE

13         %printit
SYMBOLGEN:  Macro variable SYSLAST resolves to WORK.X

NOTE: The PROCEDURE PRINT printed page 1.

MLOGIC(PRINTIT):  Ending execution.
```

Specify the MPRINT, MLOGIC, and SYMBOLGEN system options to obtain all possible information from the macro processor.

Macro Storage

Example: Successfully submit two macro definitions and print a report showing
where compiled macros are stored by default.

```
%macro reports;
   %include 'edc.macro.sascode(daily)';
   %if &sysday=Friday %then %do;
      options pageno=1;
      %include 'edc.macro.sascode(weekly)';
   %end;
%mend;

%macro printit;
   %if &syslast ne _NULL_ %then %do;
      proc print data=_last_(obs=5);
      title "Last Created Data Set Is &syslast";
      run;
   %end;
%mend;

proc catalog cat=work.sasmacr;
   contents;
   title 'Default Storage of SAS Macros';
quit;
```

PROC CATALOG Output

#	Name	Type	Date	Description
	Default Storage of SAS Macros			
	Contents of Catalog WORK.SASMACR			
1	PRINTIT	MACRO	12/22/92	
2	REPORTS	MACRO	12/22/92	

4.3 Macros with Parameters

Introduction

Suppose the compiled macro DEMO contains a reference to macro variables X and Y.

```
%macro demo;
    %if &x gt 1 %then ... ;
    %if &y gt 1 %then ... ;
%mend;
```

You can modify the behavior of DEMO by changing the value of macro variable X or Y before you call the macro.

In this first example,

```
                            Global Table
                        ┌─────────────────────┐
%let x=3;               │ X       3           │
%let y=0;               │ Y       0           │
%demo                   │                     │
                        └─────────────────────┘
```

substitutes 3 for X and 0 for Y at macro execution.

In this second example,

```
                            Global Table
                        ┌─────────────────────┐
%let x=1;               │ X       1           │
%let y=5;               │ Y       5           │
%demo                   │                     │
                        └─────────────────────┘
```

substitutes 1 for X and 5 for Y at macro execution.

Introduction

The definition of the DEMO2 macro has a *parameter list* in the **%MACRO** statement. This list contains names of macro variables referenced only within the macro.

```
%macro demo2(a,b);
    %if &a gt 1 %then ... ;
    %if &b gt 1 %then ... ;
%mend;
```

To call this macro and provide values for macro variables A and B, you can submit

```
%demo2(4,2)
```

Global Table		Local Table	
global		A	4
variables		B	2

which substitutes 4 for A and 2 for B during macro execution.

You could later submit

```
%demo2(8,0)
```

Global Table		Local Table	
global		A	8
variables		B	0

which substitutes 8 for A and 0 for B during macro execution.

Variables declared in a parameter list are always stored in a separate symbol table known as a **local table.**

By defining macros with parameter lists, you can write modular systems that

- share a common pool of macro variables (the global table)

- use an independent pool of variables (the local table) for internal processing.

Macros with Positional Parameters

You can define macros with **positional** parameters.

General form of a macro definition with positional parameters:

> **%MACRO** *macro-name(positional1, . . . , positionaln)*;
>
> > *text referencing parameter variables*
>
> **%MEND**;

Positional parameter variables in the **%MACRO** statement are

- enclosed in parentheses

- separated with commas

- stored in the local symbol table.

General form of a call to a macro defined with positional parameters:

> *%macro-name(value1, . . . , valuen)*

value1, . . . , valuen

- are enclosed in parentheses

- are separated with commas

- can be null values, text, macro variable references, or macro calls

- are substituted for the parameter variables using a one-to-one correspondence.

Note: To substitute a null value for one or more positional parameters, use commas as placeholders for the omitted values.

Macros with Positional Parameters

Example: Define a macro that creates reports showing enrollment for specific courses. Use positional parameters to specify a course and a range of dates.

```
%macro attend(crs,start,stop);
    libname perm 'edc.macro.sasdata' disp=shr;
    title1 "Course enrollment from &start to &stop";
    title2 "for All Courses";
    options pageno=1;
    proc freq data=perm.all;
       table location / nocum;
       where begin between "&start"d and "&stop"d;
    %if &crs ne %then %do;
       where also course="&crs";
       title2 "for Course &crs";
    %end;
    run;
%mend attend;
```

(handwritten margin notes: "Version 6", "Compare to (∅) or nothing")

Call the ATTEND macro twice. Print the code from each execution.

```
    options mprint mlogic;

    %attend(C003,1Jan91,31Dec91)

    %attend(,15Jun91,30Jun91)
```

Note that a null value is passed for CRS on the second call.

Macros with Positional Parameters

SAS Log from the First Macro Call

```
MLOGIC(ATTEND):  Beginning execution.
MLOGIC(ATTEND):  Parameter CRS has value C003
MLOGIC(ATTEND):  Parameter START has value 1Jan91
MLOGIC(ATTEND):  Parameter STOP has value 31Dec91
MPRINT(ATTEND):    LIBNAME PERM 'edc.macro.sasdata' DISP=SHR;
MPRINT(ATTEND):    TITLE1 "Course enrollment from 1Jan91 to 31Dec91";
MPRINT(ATTEND):    TITLE2 "for All Courses";
MPRINT(ATTEND):    OPTIONS PAGENO=1;
MPRINT(ATTEND):    PROC FREQ DATA=PERM.ALL;
MPRINT(ATTEND):    TABLE LOCATION / NOCUM;
MPRINT(ATTEND):    WHERE BEGIN BETWEEN "1Jan91"d AND "31Dec91"d;
MLOGIC(ATTEND):  %IF condition &crs ne is TRUE
MPRINT(ATTEND):    WHERE ALSO COURSE="C003";
NOTE: Where clause has been augmented.
MPRINT(ATTEND):    TITLE2 "for Course C003";
MPRINT(ATTEND):    RUN;

NOTE: The PROCEDURE FREQ printed page 1.

MLOGIC(ATTEND):  Ending execution.
```

Macros with Positional Parameters

SAS Log from the Second Macro Call

```
MLOGIC(ATTEND):  Beginning execution.
MLOGIC(ATTEND):  Parameter CRS has value
MLOGIC(ATTEND):  Parameter START has value 15Jun91
MLOGIC(ATTEND):  Parameter STOP has value 30Jun91
MPRINT(ATTEND):   LIBNAME PERM 'edc.macro.sasdata' DISP=SHR;
MPRINT(ATTEND):   TITLE1 "Course enrollment from 15Jun91 to 30Jun91";
MPRINT(ATTEND):   TITLE2 "for All Courses";
MPRINT(ATTEND):   OPTIONS PAGENO=1;
MPRINT(ATTEND):   PROC FREQ DATA=PERM.ALL;
MPRINT(ATTEND):   TABLE LOCATION / NOCUM;
MPRINT(ATTEND):   WHERE BEGIN BETWEEN "15Jun91"d AND "30Jun91"d;
MLOGIC(ATTEND):  %IF condition &crs ne is FALSE
MPRINT(ATTEND):   RUN;

NOTE: The PROCEDURE FREQ printed page 1.

MLOGIC(ATTEND):  Ending execution.
```

Macros with Keyword Parameters

You can also define macros with **keyword** parameters.

General form of a macro definition with keyword parameters:

%MACRO *macro-name(keyword=value, . . . , keyword=value)*;

      text referencing parameter variables

%MEND;

Keyword parameter variables in the **%MACRO** statement are

- enclosed in parentheses and separated with commas

- followed by an = sign

- assigned a default value (a null value is allowed)

- stored in the local symbol table.

General form of a call to a macro defined with keyword parameters:

    %macro-name(keyword=value, . . . , keyword=value) (over rode the original values)

keyword=value, . . . , keyword=value

- is enclosed in parentheses and separated with commas

- can be specified in any order

- can be omitted from the call (a keyword variable takes on its default value).

Macros with Keyword Parameters

Example: Alter the previous macro by using keyword parameters. Issue various
calls to the macro.

```
%macro attend(crs=,start=1Jan91,stop=31Dec91);
    libname perm 'edc.macro.sasdata' disp=shr;
    title1 "Course enrollment from &start to &stop";
    title2 "for All Courses";
    options pageno=1;
    proc freq data=perm.all;
        table location / nocum;
        where begin between "&start"d and "&stop"d;
    %if &crs ne %then %do;
        where also course="&crs";
        title2 "for Course &crs";
        %end;
    run;
%mend attend;

%attend(crs=C003)

%attend(start=15Jun91,stop=30Jun91)

%attend(stop=30Jun91,crs=C004)

%attend()
```

invoke the original Macro

What are the values of the omitted parameters in each call?

Macros with Mixed Parameter Lists

You can also define macros with a parameter list containing both positional and keyword parameters.

General form of a macro definition with mixed parameters:

%MACRO *macro-name(positionall, . . . , positionaln,*
keyword = value, . . . , keyword = value);

      text referencing parameter variables

%MEND;

All positional parameter variables in the **%MACRO** statement must be listed before any keyword parameter variable.

General form of a call to a macro defined with mixed parameters:

%macro-name(valuel, . . . , valuen,
keyword = value, . . . , keyword = value)

Positional values must be listed before any keyword parameter in the macro call.

Macros with Mixed Parameter Lists

Example: Alter the previous macro to make CRS a positional parameter. Leave
START and STOP as keyword parameters. Issue calls to the macro.

```
%macro attend(crs,start=1JAN91,stop=31DEC91);
   libname perm 'edc.macro.sasdata' disp=shr;
   title1 "Course enrollment from &start to &stop";
   title2 "for All Courses";
   options pageno=1;
   proc freq data=perm.all;
      table location / nocum;
      where begin between "&start"d and "&stop"d;
   %if &crs ne %then %do;
      where also course="&crs";
      title2 "for Course &crs";
   %end;
   run;
%mend attend;

%attend(C008)

%attend(start=1Jun91)

%attend(C002,stop=31May91)

%attend()

%attend

%attend;
```

Note: For macros defined with a parameter list, the token after *%macro-name*
triggers macro execution. The call **%attend** is executed when the **%** of the
next call is encountered. The semicolon after the last call triggers macro
execution and submits a null statement. Using a semicolon to trigger
macro execution can cause problems if the macro does not generate SAS
statements.

In interactive SAS sessions, submitting only **%attend** does not trigger
macro execution.

4.4 Global and Local Symbol Tables

Introduction

When you write applications using SAS macros, you can have multiple symbol tables available to store macro variables, the **global** table and one or more **local** tables.

This section discusses

- creation and deletion of symbol tables

- relationships among symbol tables

- ways of creating macro variables in a specific table

- how to make sure the appropriate table is used when a macro variable reference is made.

The Global Symbol Table

The global symbol table is

- created during the initialization of a SAS session or noninteractive execution

- initialized with automatic or system-defined macro variables

- deleted at the end of the session.

Macro variables in the global symbol table

- are available anytime during the session

- can be created by your program

- have values that can be changed during the session (except some automatic macro variables)

- cannot be removed once they are created (they can be assigned a null value).

```
        Global Symbol Table

   ┌─────────────────────────────┐
   │ Variable    Value           │
   ├─────────────────────────────┤
   │ SYSDATE     24OCT91         │
   │ SYSDAY      Thursday        │
   │ SYSVER      6.07            │
   │    .           .            │
   │    .           .            │
   │    .           .            │
   │ uservar1    value1          │
   │ uservar2    value2          │
   └─────────────────────────────┘
```

The Global Symbol Table

You can create a global macro variable with a

- %LET statement (used outside a macro definition)

- DATA step containing a SYMPUT routine

- SELECT statement containing an INTO clause in PROC SQL

- %GLOBAL statement.

General form of the %GLOBAL statement:

%GLOBAL *macrovar1   macrovar2* . . . ;

The **%GLOBAL** statement

- creates one or more macro variables in the global symbol table and assigns them null values

- can be used inside or outside a macro definition

- has no effect on variables already in the global table.

The Local Symbol Table

A local symbol table is

- created when a macro with a parameter list is called or a request is made to create a local variable during macro execution

- deleted when the macro finishes execution.

The local symbol table contains macro variables that can be

- created and initialized at macro invocation (parameters)

- created during macro execution

- updated during macro execution

- referenced anywhere within the macro.

```
          Local Symbol Table

      ┌─────────────────────────────┐
      │  Variable      Value        │
      │─────────────────────────────│
      │                             │
      │  parameter1    value1       │
      │  parameter2    value2       │
      │      .             .        │
      │      .             .        │
      │      .             .        │
      │  uservar1      value1       │
      │  uservar2      value2       │
      └─────────────────────────────┘
```

The Local Symbol Table

Besides macro parameters, you can create local macro variables with a

- **%LET** statement

- DATA step containing a SYMPUT routine

- SELECT statement containing an INTO clause in PROC SQL

- **%LOCAL** statement

used **inside** a macro definition.

General form of the **%LOCAL** statement:

> **%LOCAL** *macrovar1   macrovar2* . . . ;

The **%LOCAL** statement

- can appear only inside a macro definition

- creates one or more macro variables in the local symbol table and assigns them null values

- has no effect on variables already in the local table.

Note: A local table is not created until a request is made to create a local variable. Macros that do not create local variables do not have a local table.

Rules for Creating and Updating Variables

When the macro processor receives a request to create or update a macro variable **during a macro call**, the macro processor follows these rules:

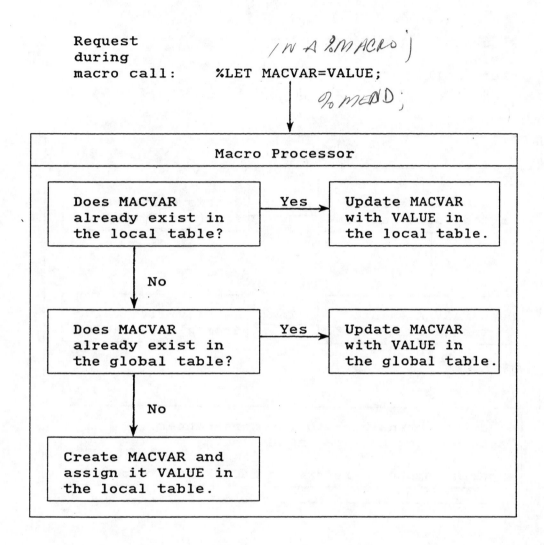

```
Request
during
macro call:          %LET MACVAR=VALUE;
```

IN A %MACRO)

% MEND ;

```
┌─────────────────────────────────────────────────────────────┐
│                      Macro Processor                         │
│                                                              │
│  ┌──────────────────────┐   Yes   ┌──────────────────────┐  │
│  │ Does MACVAR          │────────▶│ Update MACVAR        │  │
│  │ already exist in     │         │ with VALUE in        │  │
│  │ the local table?     │         │ the local table.     │  │
│  └──────────────────────┘         └──────────────────────┘  │
│             │                                                │
│             │ No                                             │
│             ▼                                                │
│  ┌──────────────────────┐   Yes   ┌──────────────────────┐  │
│  │ Does MACVAR          │────────▶│ Update MACVAR        │  │
│  │ already exist in     │         │ with VALUE in        │  │
│  │ the global table?    │         │ the global table.    │  │
│  └──────────────────────┘         └──────────────────────┘  │
│             │                                                │
│             │ No                                             │
│             ▼                                                │
│  ┌──────────────────────┐                                   │
│  │ Create MACVAR and    │                                   │
│  │ assign it VALUE in   │                                   │
│  │ the local table.     │                                   │
│  └──────────────────────┘                                   │
└─────────────────────────────────────────────────────────────┘
```

Rules for Resolving Variables

In order to resolve a macro variable reference **during a macro call,** the macro processor follows these rules:

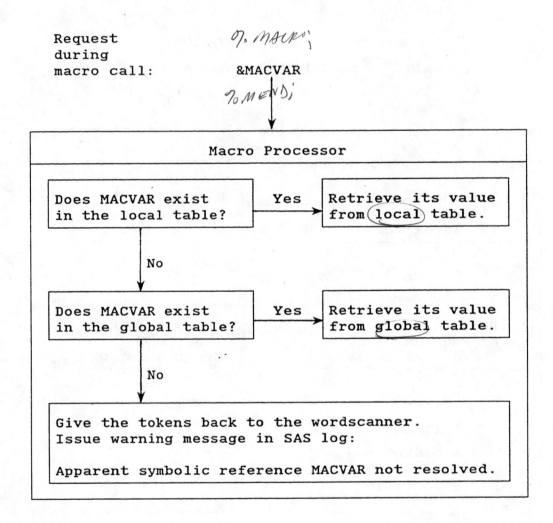

Relationships among Global and Local Tables

Example: The WHOAMI macro uses a %LET statement to create a macro
variable NAME based on the global macro variable SYSJOBID.

```
%macro whoami;
    %if &sysjobid=ABC01 %then %let name=Moe;
    %else %if &sysjobid=ABC02 %then %let name=Jo;
    %else %if &sysjobid=ABC03 %then %let name=Flo;
    %else %let name=Unknown Person;
%mend;
```

Suppose you call the WHOAMI macro. The NAME variable is created in the
local table.

	Global Table	Local Table
%whoami	SYSJOBID ABC02	NAME Jo

After macro execution, you submit a TITLE statement for a report:

```
title "Report run by &name";
```

What title text would appear in the report?

Relationships among Global and Local Tables

Example: Define NAME as a global variable. Re-execute the WHOAMI macro.

```
%macro whoami;
    %if &sysjobid=ABC01 %then %let name=Moe;
    %else %if &sysjobid=ABC02 %then %let name=Jo;
    %else %if &sysjobid=ABC03 %then %let name=Flo;
    %else %let name=Unknown Person;
%mend;
```

                                  Global Table

```
(%global name;)         ┌─────────────────────┐
%whoami                 │ SYSJOBID ABC02      │
                        │ NAME     Jo         │
                        └─────────────────────┘
```

or
next
page

After macro execution, you submit the TITLE statement for a report:

```
title "Report run by &name";
```

What title text would appear in the report?

Relationships among Global and Local Tables

You can use a **%GLOBAL** statement in a macro definition if

- you are not sure what variables are in the global table when the macro executes

- you want to guarantee that a **%LET** statement updates a global variable.

```
%macro whoami;
   %global name;
      %if &sysjobid=ABC01 %then %let name=Moe;
      %else %if &sysjobid=ABC02 %then %let name=Jo;
      %else %if &sysjobid=ABC03 %then %let name=Flo;
      %else %let name=Unknown Person;
%mend;

%whoami
title "Report run by &name";
```

Local table Does not exist here!

Relationships among Global and Local Tables

You should use a **%LOCAL** statement in a macro definition to

- avoid accidentally updating the global table during macro execution

- guarantee that a **%LET** statement updates a local variable.

```
%macro whoami;
   %local name;
   %if &sysjobid=ABC01 %then %let name=Moe;
   %else %if &sysjobid=ABC02 %then %let name=Jo;
   %else %if &sysjobid=ABC03 %then %let name=Flo;
   %else %let name=;
   %if &name ne %then %str(title "Report run by &name";);
%mend;
```

Global table

```
%let name=Davis;
```

Global Table

SYSJOBID	ABC02
NAME	Davis

```
%whoami
```

Local Table

NAME	Jo

```
proc print data=perm.students;
   where name ? "&name";
run;
```

contains

What TITLE statement is submitted? *"Report run by Jo"*

What WHERE statement is submitted?

Where name contains "DAVIS";
(?)

What code would have been submitted if the %LOCAL statement were omitted?

NAME DAVIS change NAME =JO resolves to Jo every time

For=ABC02

Creating Variables with SYMPUT and INTO

Rule: During the execution of a macro, macro variables created with the DATA
step SYMPUT routine or the INTO clause in PROC SQL are placed in
the local symbol table, if the local table already exists. Otherwise, they are
placed in the global table.

Example: Use the NUMOBS macro to determine the number of nondeleted
observations in any SAS data set (excluding views).

NUMOBS Macro

```
%macro numobs;
   proc sql noprint;
      select (nobs-delobs) into: num
      from dictionary.tables
      where libname="&lib" and memname="&dsn";
   %let num=&num;
   quit;
%mend;
```

A Call to the NUMOBS Macro

```
%let lib=PERM;
%let dsn=REGISTER;

%numobs

title "Total Registered Students is &num";
```

Partial SAS Log

```
14          %numobs
SYMBOLGEN:  Macro variable LIB resolves to PERM
SYMBOLGEN:  Macro variable DSN resolves to REGISTER
SYMBOLGEN:  Macro variable NUM resolves to      434
NOTE: The PROCEDURE SQL used 0.06 CPU seconds and 1906K.

SYMBOLGEN:  Macro variable NUM resolves to 434
15
16          title "Total Registered Students is &num";
```

Creating Variables with SYMPUT and INTO

If the local table already exists, the SYMPUT routine or INTO clause creates local variables.

Revised NUMOBS Macro with Parameters

```
%macro numobs(lib,dsn);
   proc sql noprint;
      select (nobs-delobs) into: num
      from dictionary.tables
      where libname="&lib" and memname="&dsn";
   %let num=&num;
   quit;
%mend;
```

A Call to the NUMOBS Macro

```
%numobs(PERM,REGISTER)

title "Total Enrollment is &num";
```

Partial SAS Log

```
11         %numobs(PERM,REGISTER)
SYMBOLGEN:  Macro variable LIB resolves to PERM
SYMBOLGEN:  Macro variable DSN resolves to REGISTER
SYMBOLGEN:  Macro variable NUM resolves to      434
NOTE: The PROCEDURE SQL used 0.06 CPU seconds and 1910K.

WARNING: Apparent symbolic reference NUM not resolved.
12
13         title "Total Enrollment is &num";
```

Creating Variables with SYMPUT and INTO

You can create variables with the **%GLOBAL** statement and then use the SYMPUT routine or INTO clause to update these variables during macro execution when the local table exists.

NUMOBS Macro with Parameters

Local

Places Forced

```
%macro numobs(lib,dsn);
   %global num;
   %let num=0;
   proc sql noprint;
      select (nobs-delobs) into :num
      from dictionary.tables
      where libname="&lib" and memname="&dsn";
   %let num=&num;
   quit;
%mend;
```

A Call to the NUMOBS Macro

where incorrect name used   *resetting the num=0*

```
%numobs(PERM,REGISTER)
```

Don't get wrong # in NUM

```
title "Total Enrollment is &num";
```

Partial SAS Log

```
13          %numobs(PERM,REGISTER)
SYMBOLGEN:  Macro variable LIB resolves to PERM
SYMBOLGEN:  Macro variable DSN resolves to REGISTER
SYMBOLGEN:  Macro variable NUM resolves to        434
NOTE: The PROCEDURE SQL used 0.07 CPU seconds and 1902K.

SYMBOLGEN:  Macro variable NUM resolves to 434
14
15          title "Total Enrollment is &num";
```

Note: See Appendix B for more information about dictionary tables.

Multiple Local Tables

Multiple local tables can exist concurrently during macro execution.

Example: Define two macros. Call one within the other.

```
%macro outer;
    %local x;
    %let x=1;
    %inner
%mend outer;

%macro inner;
    %local y;
    %let y=&x;
%mend inner;
```

When the OUTER macro is called, a local table is created for it. The diagram shows the state of the symbol tables before the INNER macro is called.

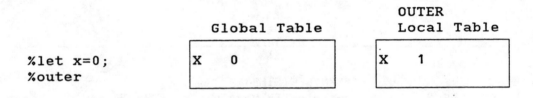

```
                        Global Table          OUTER
                                              Local Table

%let x=0;              ┌─────────────┐       ┌─────────────┐
%outer                 │ X     0     │       │ X     1     │
                       └─────────────┘       └─────────────┘
```

What would be in the symbol tables if the **%LOCAL** statement in the OUTER macro is omitted?

Multiple Local Tables

Rule: A nested macro call can create its own local symbol table. This table is in
addition to any other tables that may currently exist.

```
%macro outer;
    %local x;
    %let x=1;
    %inner
%mend outer;

%macro inner;
    %local y;
    %let y=&x;    x =(1)
%mend inner;
```

The diagram shows the state of the symbol tables after the %LOCAL statement in
the INNER macro is executed.

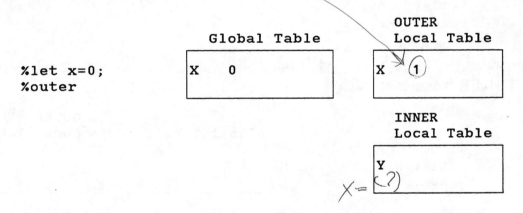

```
%let x=0;
%outer
```

Multiple Local Tables

Rule: The macro processor resolves a macro variable reference by searching
symbol tables in the reverse order in which they were created:

1. current local table

2. previously created local tables

3. global table

```
%macro outer;
    %local x;
    %let x=1;
    %inner
%mend outer;

%macro inner;
    %local y;
    %let y=&x;
%mend inner;
```

The diagram shows the state of the symbol tables after the **%LET** statement in the
INNER macro is executed.

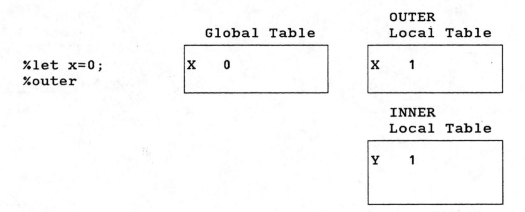

```
%let x=0;
%outer
```

The global variable X is not available to the INNER macro.

Multiple Local Tables

Once the INNER macro finishes execution, its local table is removed. Control passes back to the OUTER macro.

```
%macro outer;
    %local x;
    %let x=1;
    %inner
%mend outer;

%macro inner;
    %local y;
    %let y=&x;
%mend inner;
```

This diagram shows the state of the symbol tables after the INNER macro is executed.

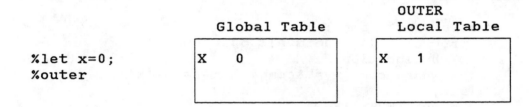

```
%let x=0;
%outer
```

	Global Table		OUTER Local Table
	X 0		X 1

This diagram shows the state of the symbol tables after the OUTER macro is executed.

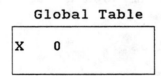

	Global Table
	X 0

Multiple Local Tables

Example: Call the NUMOBS macro within another macro to find the number of
observations in a subsetted data set. Conditionally execute additional
SAS code if the subsetted data set contains observations.

NUMOBS Macro

```
%macro numobs(lib,dsn);
    %global num;
    %let num=0;
    proc sql noprint;
        select (nobs-delobs) into: num
        from dictionary.tables
        where libname="&lib" and memname="&dsn";
    %let num=&num;
    quit;
%mend;
```

CHECK Macro

```
%macro check(comp);
    proc sort data=perm.all out=temp;
        by location;
        where company="&comp" and paid='N';
    run;
    %numobs(WORK,TEMP)
    %if &num>0 %then %do;
        proc print data=temp noobs;
            by location;
            var name title fee begin;
            sum fee;
            title "&num Unpaid Students from &comp";
        run;
    %end;
    %else %str(endsas;);
%mend;
```

What changes would you make to these macros to make NUM a local variable in
the symbol table for CHECK?

Multiple Local Tables

A Call to the CHECK Macro

```
%check(Reston Railway)
```

Partial SAS Log

```
MPRINT(CHECK):    PROC SORT DATA=PERM.ALL OUT=TEMP;
MPRINT(CHECK):    BY LOCATION;
MPRINT(CHECK):    WHERE COMPANY="Reston Railway" AND PAID='N';
MPRINT(CHECK):    RUN;

NOTE: The data set WORK.TEMP has 14 observations and 12 variables.

MPRINT(NUMOBS):    PROC SQL NOPRINT;
MPRINT(NUMOBS):    SELECT (NOBS-DELOBS) INTO: NUM FROM
DICTIONARY.TABLES WHERE LIBNAME="WORK" AND MEMNAME="TEMP";
MPRINT(NUMOBS):    QUIT;

MPRINT(CHECK):    PROC PRINT DATA=TEMP NOOBS;
MPRINT(CHECK):    BY LOCATION;
MPRINT(CHECK):    VAR NAME TITLE FEE BEGIN;
MPRINT(CHECK):    SUM FEE;
MPRINT(CHECK):    TITLE "14 Unpaid Students from Reston Railway";
MPRINT(CHECK):    RUN;
```

Multiple Local Tables

Another Call to the CHECK Macro

```
%check(Raston Railway)
```

Partial SAS Log

```
MPRINT(CHECK):    PROC SORT DATA=PERM.ALL OUT=TEMP;
MPRINT(CHECK):    BY LOCATION;
MPRINT(CHECK):    WHERE COMPANY="Raston Railway" AND PAID='N';
MPRINT(CHECK):    RUN;

NOTE: The data set WORK.TEMP has 0 observations and 12 variables.

MPRINT(NUMOBS):    PROC SQL NOPRINT;
MPRINT(NUMOBS):    SELECT (NOBS-DELOBS) INTO: NUM FROM
DICTIONARY.TABLES WHERE LIBNAME="WORK" AND MEMNAME="TEMP";
MPRINT(NUMOBS):    QUIT;

NOTE: SAS Institute Inc., SAS Campus Drive, Cary, NC USA 27513-2414
```

Note: Most SAS steps that read empty data sets do not produce output or
        generate worthless results. By terminating a SAS program prematurely,
        you eliminate the CPU time spent in compiling the remainder of the
        program.

Tips on Writing Macro Programs

Many SAS programmers develop macros as follows:

1. If a macro is used to generate SAS code, write and debug the desired SAS program without any macro coding. Make sure the SAS program runs with hard-coded programming constants on a fixed set of data.

2. Generalize the program by removing hard-coded programming constants and substituting macro variable references. Initialize the macro variables with **%LET** statements and try different values for the macro variables. Use the SYMBOLGEN system option to assist in debugging or confirmation. You may need to adjust the basic program to make it more generalized.

3. Create a macro definition by inserting **%MACRO** and **%MEND** statements around your program. Convert **%LET** statements to macro parameters, if desired. Decide on the scope of all macro variables (global or local) and declare accordingly. Call the macro using different parameter values. Use the MPRINT and SYMBOLGEN system options for debugging.

4. Add macro-level programming statements such as **%IF-%THEN** after the macro executes successfully. Thoroughly test any macro-level programming logic. Use the MLOGIC and SYMBOLGEN system options for debugging.

This process allows rapid development and debugging because you are isolating syntax and logic at the SAS code level from the syntax and logic at the macro level.

LIBNAME PERM 'SYS3.SAS6.WORKSHOP.
SASDATA' DISP=SHR;

4.5 Exercises

4.1   Defining, Executing, and Debugging a Macro

a.   If you have a display manager session active, issue the BYE command
to exit it. Start a new session. Include the program C4EX1 shown
below into the PROGRAM EDITOR window and submit it.

```
%macro printit;
   %if &syslast=_NULL_   %then %do;
      proc print data=_last_(obs=5);
          title "Last Created Data Set Is &syslast";
      run;
   end;
%mend;
```

Use the SAS log to diagnose the compilation error. Recall the
program and fix the syntax error. Resubmit the macro definition.

Symbolgen
MLOGIC

M

b.   Submit a call to the PRINTIT macro. You should get an error
message. Activate system options that print information in the SAS
log to help you diagnose the error. Call the PRINTIT macro again
and examine the SAS log. Fix the logic error in the program.
Resubmit the macro definition and call the macro. If no SAS code is
submitted when the macro is called, you have repaired the error.

c.   Alter the macro definition by adding a statement that executes this
statement whenever the %IF expression is false:

```
%put No SAS data set has been created.;
```

Recompile the macro and call it. The text from the %PUT statement
should appear in the SAS log.

d.   Submit this program:

```
proc sort data=perm.students out=business nodupkey;
   by company;
run;
```

LIBNAME

Make a call to the PRINTIT macro. You should get a partial listing
of the BUSINESS data set.

INC 'SYS3.SAS6.WORKSHOP.SASCODE(C4EX1)

Exercises

4.2   Defining and Using a Macro Parameter

a.   Redefine the PRINTIT macro so it accepts a positional parameter NUM, the number of observations to print. Change the coding in the macro so it references NUM. Submit the new definition.

b.   Call the PRINTIT macro twice, using values of 10 and 20 for NUM.

4.3   Using Positional and Keyword Parameters

This exercise involves using a PROC FREQ step to perform crosstabulations. The following is the general form of a PROC FREQ step for your reference:

PROC FREQ DATA = *SAS-data-set*;
    TABLES *(row-vars)* * *(column-vars)* | *options*;
RUN:

a.   Include the program C4EX3 shown below into the PROGRAM EDITOR window, submit it, and view the output.

```
                          DS N
    proc freq data=perm.register;
        tables (paid) / nocum;
    run;            Y            (OPTION)
                    N
```

b.   Recall the program and alter it so that the PROC FREQ step is generated by a macro named COUNTS. Replace the hard-coded data set name, column name, and option in the PROC FREQ code with macro variable references. The macro variables should be parameters of the COUNTS macro and are described below.

    COLS   defines the column variables of the table.
    DSN   defines the SAS data set used.
    OPT   defines options for the TABLES statement.

    COLS should be a positional parameter. Values for this parameter can be variable names separated by blanks.

    DSN should be a keyword parameter with a default value of `_last_`.

    OPT should be a keyword parameter with a null default value.

Exercises

4.3   Using Positional and Keyword Parameters (continued)

Submit the COUNTS macro definition. Call the COUNTS macro using the PERM.REGISTER data set to create a simple frequency table for PAID (column variable). Supply the NOCUM option to suppress the printing of cumulative statistics.

c.   Recall the macro definition and alter it so that the COUNTS macro conditionally submits the step based on at least one column variable being supplied on the call. If the value of COLS is null, no code should be submitted.   %IF &cols ne _ ~other~null~

Include a TITLE statement in COUNTS that indicates the SAS data set being used and the date submitted. Include an OPTIONS statement specifying the NODATE and NONUMBER system options.

Submit the new COUNTS macro definition. Call the COUNTS macro using the PERM.REGISTER data set and no other parameters.

d.   **(Optional)**

Recall the macro definition and alter it to add a second positional parameter named ROWS. This macro variable defines the row variables of the table.

TABLES . Rows (OPTIONAL)

Alter the logic of the COUNTS macro such that if the ROWS macro variable has a value, then the submitted TABLES statement should include the row variables, the parentheses around the row variables, and the following asterisk.

Submit the macro definition and then call the COUNTS macro using the PERM.ALL data set to create a crosstabulation using COURSE as the column variable and PAID as the row variable.

e.   **(Optional)**

Call the COUNTS macro using the PERM.ALL data set to create two crosstabulations. Use COURSE and LOCATION as column variables. Use PAID as the row variable. Supply the NOROW and NOCOL options.

Exercises

4.4   Creating Multiple Symbol Tables

a.   The DATA step shown below creates a macro variable named
TODAY that contains today's date in the MMDDYY8. format.

```
data _null_;
    call symput('today',put(today(),mmddyy8.));
run;
```

Write a macro named MAKEDATE that contains the DATA step.
Specify one positional parameter named FMT and change the
MMDDYY8. format in the DATA step to &fmt. Submit the macro
definition.

b.   Recall the definition for the COUNTS macro (Exercise 4.3) and
replace the reference to the SYSDATE variable in the TITLE
statement with a reference to the TODAY variable. Include a call to
the MAKEDATE macro within the COUNTS macro prior to the
TITLE statement. Specify mmddyy10. for the FMT parameter.

c.   Submit the definition for the COUNTS macro and make a call to it.
Note that the TODAY variable does not resolve. Why?

Recall the definition of the COUNTS macro and add a statement that
makes TODAY a local variable. Submit the definition. Call the
COUNTS macro again. The TITLE statement should contain today's
date in MMDDYY10. format.

4.6 Chapter Summary

You can use SAS macro programs to execute macro statements or submit SAS code conditionally.

A macro definition (macro) consists of **%MACRO** and **%MEND** statements that serve to mark the beginning and end of the macro definition. The **%MACRO** statement also provides a name for the macro. Any combination of macro and SAS code can be placed between these statements as part of the macro definition. Some macro statements such as **%IF** and **%DO** can be coded only within a macro definition. The macro definition must be submitted before you can execute the macro.

To execute a defined macro, submit the name of macro preceded by a percent sign. This is not a SAS statement and the macro call does not require a semicolon to execute. Once a macro is defined, it can be called many times within the same SAS execution.

When a macro executes, it may create its own temporary symbol table called a local table. If a macro creates or resolves macro variables, two or more symbol tables may be used. You must understand the basic rules governing which symbol tables are accessed under given circumstances to fully control macro behavior. **%LOCAL** and **%GLOBAL** statements enable you to explicitly define where macro variables are stored. You can call a macro within a macro definition (nesting). When a nested macro is called, there may be multiple local symbol tables available.

To make macros more flexible, you can define a parameter list as part of the **%MACRO** statement. The parameter can be either positional or keyword. These parameters define local macro variables that can take on different values when you call the macro.

Two system options, MLOGIC and MPRINT, are useful for macro development and debugging. The MLOGIC system option writes messages to the SAS log tracing macro execution. The MPRINT system option prints the SAS code ultimately sent to the compiler after all macro resolution has taken place.

Chapter Summary

General form of a simple macro definition:

%MACRO *macro-name*;
　　　macro-text
%MEND *macro-name*;

General form of a macro call:

%macro-name

General form of **%IF-%THEN** and **%ELSE** statements:

%IF *expression* **%THEN** *text*;

%ELSE *text*;

General form of **%DO** and **%END** statements:

%IF *expression* **%THEN** **%DO**;
　　　statement; statement; . . .
%END;

%ELSE %DO;
　　　statement; statement; . . .
%END;

System options:

MPRINT|NOMPRINT
MLOGIC|NOMLOGIC

General form of a macro definition with positional parameters:

%MACRO *macro-name(positional1, . . . , positionaln)*;

　　　text referencing parameter variables

%MEND;

Chapter Summary

General form of a call to a macro defined with positional parameters:

   %*macro-name(value1, . . . , valuen)*

General form of a macro definition with keyword parameters:

   %MACRO *macro-name(keyword=value, . . . , keyword=value)*;

      text referencing parameter variables

   %MEND;

General form of a call to a macro defined with keyword parameters:

   %*macro-name(keyword=value, . . . , keyword=value)*

General form of a macro definition with mixed parameters:

   %MACRO *macro-name(positional1, . . . , positionaln,
                    keyword=value, . . . , keyword=value)*;

      text referencing parameter variables

   %MEND;

General form of a call to a macro defined with mixed parameters:

   %*macro-name(value1, . . . , valuen,
                    keyword=value, . . . , keyword=value)*

General form of the **%GLOBAL** statement:

   %GLOBAL *macrovar1 macrovar2 . . .* ;

General form of the **%LOCAL** statement:

   %LOCAL *macrovar1 macrovar2 . . .* ;

4.7 Solutions and Selected Output

4.1   Defining, Executing, and Debugging a Macro

a.   The compilation error is caused by the missing percent sign in the %END statement.

b.

```
options mlogic symbolgen mprint;
%printit
```

The operator used with the **%IF** statement should be **ne** not **=** .

```
%macro printit;
   %if &syslast ne _NULL_  %then %do;
      proc print data=_last_(obs=5);
         title "Last Created Data Set Is &syslast";
      run;
   %end;
%mend;
```

Solutions and Selected Output

4.1   Defining, Executing, and Debugging a Macro (continued)

c.

```
%macro printit;
    %if &syslast ne _NULL_  %then %do;
        proc print data=_last_(obs=5);
            title "Last Created Data Set Is &syslast";
        run;
    %end;
    %else %put No SAS data set has been created.;
%mend;
```

Alternate Solution:

```
%macro printit;
    %if &syslast=_NULL_ %then
        %put No SAS data set has been created.;
    %else %do;
        proc print data=_last_(obs=5);
            title "Last Created Data Set Is &syslast";
        run;
    %end;
%mend;
```

Solutions and Selected Output

4.2   Defining and Using a Macro Parameter

a.

```
%macro printit(num);
   %if &syslast ne _NULL_  %then %do;
      proc print data=_last_(obs=&num);
         title "Last Created Data Set Is &syslast";
      run;
   %end;
   %else %put No SAS data set has been created.;
%mend;
```

b.

```
%printit(10)
%printit(20)
```

Solutions and Selected Output

4.3   Using Positional and Keyword Parameters

b.

```
%macro counts(cols,dsn=_last_,opt=);
   proc freq data=&dsn;
      tables (&cols) / &opt;
   run;
%mend counts;
%counts(paid,dsn=perm.register,opt=nocum)
```

```
                    The SAS System

                    Paid Status

        PAID   Frequency    Percent
        -----------------------------
        N          107        24.7
        Y          327        75.3
```

c.

```
%macro counts(cols,dsn=_last_,opt=);
   %if &cols ne %then %do;
      title "Report on &dsn Created &sysdate";
      options nodate nonumber;
      proc freq data=&dsn;
         tables (&cols) / &opt;
      run;
   %end;
%mend counts;
%counts(dsn=perm.register)
```

No output generated.

Solutions and Selected Output

4.3   Using Positional and Keyword Parameters (continued)

d.

```
%macro counts(cols,rows,dsn=_last_,opt=);
   %if &cols ne %then %do;
      title "Report on &dsn Created &sysdate";
      options nodate nonumber;
      proc freq data=&dsn;
         tables
      %if &rows ne %then (&rows) *;
         (&cols) / &opt;
      run;
   %end;
%mend counts;
%counts(course,paid,dsn=perm.all)
```

Solutions and Selected Output

4.3   Using Positional and Keyword Parameters (continued)

d.

Output

```
                    Report on perm.all Created 02OCT92

                     TABLE OF PAID BY COURSE

PAID(Paid Status)        COURSE(Course Code)

Frequency|
Percent  |
Row Pct  |
Col Pct  |C001    |C002    |C003    |C004    |C005    |C006    |  Total
---------+--------+--------+--------+--------+--------+--------+
N        |     14 |     20 |     19 |     17 |     24 |     13 |    107
         |   3.23 |   4.61 |   4.38 |   3.92 |   5.53 |   3.00 |  24.65
         |  13.08 |  18.69 |  17.76 |  15.89 |  22.43 |  12.15 |
         |  20.29 |  25.97 |  25.68 |  22.08 |  33.80 |  19.70 |
---------+--------+--------+--------+--------+--------+--------+
Y        |     55 |     57 |     55 |     60 |     47 |     53 |    327
         |  12.67 |  13.13 |  12.67 |  13.82 |  10.83 |  12.21 |  75.35
         |  16.82 |  17.43 |  16.82 |  18.35 |  14.37 |  16.21 |
         |  79.71 |  74.03 |  74.32 |  77.92 |  66.20 |  80.30 |
---------+--------+--------+--------+--------+--------+--------+
Total          69       77       74       77       71       66      434
            15.90    17.74    17.05    17.74    16.36    15.21   100.00
```

Solutions and Selected Output

4.3   Using Positional and Keyword Parameters (continued)

e.

```
%counts(course location,paid,
        dsn=perm.all,opt=norow nocol)
```

Partial Output

```
                    Report on perm.all Created 02OCT92

                        TABLE OF PAID BY COURSE

    PAID(Paid Status)       COURSE(Course Code)

    Frequency|
    Percent  |C001    |C002    |C003    |C004    |C005    |C006    | Total
    ---------+--------+--------+--------+--------+--------+--------+
    N        |    14 |     20 |     19 |     17 |     24 |     13 |    107
```

```
                    Report on perm.all Created 02OCT92

                        TABLE OF PAID BY LOCATION

    PAID(Paid Status)        LOCATION(Location)

    Frequency|
    Percent  |Boston  |Dallas  |Seattle |  Total
    ---------+--------+--------+--------+
    N        |    33 |     46 |     28 |    107
```

Solutions and Selected Output

4.4   Creating Multiple Symbol Tables

a.

```
%macro makedate(fmt);
    data _null_;
        call symput('today',put(today(),&fmt));
    run;
%mend;
```

b.

```
%macro counts(cols,rows,dsn=_last_,opt=);
    %if &cols ne %then %do;
        %makedate(mmddyy10.)
        title "Report on &dsn Created &today";
        options nodate nonumber;
        proc freq data=&dsn;
            tables %if &rows ne %then (&rows) *;
                    (&cols) / &opt;
        run;
    %end;
%mend counts;
```

c.

```
%counts(paid,dsn=perm.register,opt=nocum)
```

```
             Report on perm.register Created &today

                      Paid Status

            PAID   Frequency   Percent
            ---------------------------
            N           107      24.7
            Y           327      75.3
```

Solutions and Selected Output

4.4   Creating Multiple Symbol Tables (continued)

    c.   (continued)

The macro variable TODAY is a local variable to the MAKEDATE table, which is subordinate to the COUNTS table. TODAY cannot be resolved in the COUNTS macro.

Corrected macro

```
%macro counts(cols,rows,dsn=_last_,opt=);
   %if &cols ne %then %do;
      %local today;
      %makedate(mmddyy10.)
      title "Report on &dsn Created &today";
      options nodate nonumber;
      proc freq data=&dsn;
         tables %if &rows ne %then (&rows) *;
                (&cols) / &opt;
      run;
   %end;
%mend counts;


%counts(paid,dsn=perm.register,opt=nocum)
```

Output from Corrected Macro

```
Report on perm.register Created 09/23/1992

          Paid Status

PAID   Frequency   Percent
-----------------------------
N         107        24.7
Y         327        75.3
```

5. Macro Applications

5.1 Manipulating Character Strings

5.2 Iterative Processing

5.3 Arithmetic and Logical Operations

5.4 More about %EVAL and Macro Quoting (Optional)

5.5 Exercises

5.6 Chapter Summary

5.7 Solutions and Selected Output

5.1 Manipulating Character Strings

Introduction

Many macro applications require character string manipulation.

Selected macro character functions:

%UPCASE   translates letters from lowercase to uppercase.

%LENGTH   determines the length of a character string.

%SUBSTR   produces a substring of a character string.

%SCAN   extracts a word from a character string.

%INDEX   finds the position of the first occurrence of a character string within another string.

Macro functions share the same basic syntax as the corresponding DATA step functions and yield similar results.

Note: All macro functions can be used inside or outside macro definitions.

Case of Text Issues

Most comparison operators in the SAS language are case sensitive.

Example: Create a listing of all students from a company named Smash by assigning the value **Smash** to the automatic macro variable SYSPARM and submitting the program below.

```
proc print data=perm.students noobs;
   where company ? "&sysparm";
   title "Students from &sysparm";
run;
```

```
                       Students from Smash

          NAME                  COMPANY              CITYST

      Taylor, Mr. Greg     Smash Consulting      Decatur, IL
```

Suppose you assigned the value **SMASH** to the SYSPARM variable. The report is shown below.

```
                       Students from SMASH

          NAME                  COMPANY              CITYST

      Parker, Mr. Robert    SMASH Hardware Inc.   Bozeman, MT
      Valeri, Mr. Marshall  SMASH Hardware Inc.   Bozeman, MT
      Voboril, Mr. Jim      SMASH Hardware Inc.   Bozeman, MT
```

Note: The WHERE clause sounds-like operator (= *) is not case sensitive.

Case of Text Issues

To ensure the matching of values when case is not important, use the UPCASE function to translate data values to uppercase before making comparisons.

SYSPARM has the value SMASH for the program below.

```
proc print data=perm.students noobs;
   where upcase(company) ? "&sysparm";
   title "Students from &sysparm";
run;
```

```
                     Students from SMASH

        NAME                    COMPANY            CITYST

    Parker, Mr. Robert      SMASH Hardware Inc.    Bozeman, MT
    Taylor, Mr. Greg        Smash Consulting       Decatur, IL
    Valeri, Mr. Marshall    SMASH Hardware Inc.    Bozeman, MT
    Voboril, Mr. Jim        SMASH Hardware Inc.    Bozeman, MT
```

What would happen if this program is run when SYSPARM has the value Smash?

Case of Text Issues

You might need to translate the value of a macro variable to uppercase before

- making comparisons at the macro level

- substituting its value in a SAS program.

The %UPCASE function translates all letters in its argument to uppercase. Other characters are unaffected.

Example: Use the FINDER macro to create a listing of students from a specified company.

```
%macro finder(value,case=asis);
   %if %upcase(&case)=ASIS %then %do;
      proc print data=perm.students noobs;
         where company ? "&value";
         title "Students from &value";
      run;
   %end;
   %else %if %upcase(&case)=ANY %then %do;
      proc print data=perm.students noobs;
         where upcase(company) ? "%upcase(&value)";
         title "Students from &value";
      run;
   %end;
%mend;
```

SYSPARM has the value SMASH for the macro call below.

```
%finder(&sysparm)
```

```
                    Students from SMASH

         NAME                 COMPANY            CITYST

    Parker, Mr. Robert    SMASH Hardware Inc.   Bozeman, MT
    Valeri, Mr. Marshall  SMASH Hardware Inc.   Bozeman, MT
    Voboril, Mr. Jim      SMASH Hardware Inc.   Bozeman, MT
```

Case of Text Issues

SYSPARM has the value `Smash` for the macro call below.

```
%finder(&sysparm)
```

```
                  Students from Smash

     NAME              COMPANY            CITYST

 Taylor, Mr. Greg    Smash Consulting    Decatur, IL
```

SYSPARM has the value `Smash` for the macro call below.

```
%finder(&sysparm,case=any)
```

```
                    Students from Smash

      NAME                 COMPANY            CITYST

 Parker, Mr. Robert     SMASH Hardware Inc.   Bozeman, MT
 Taylor, Mr. Greg       Smash Consulting      Decatur, IL
 Valeri, Mr. Marshall   SMASH Hardware Inc.   Bozeman, MT
 Voboril, Mr. Jim       SMASH Hardware Inc.   Bozeman, MT
```

Note: You can also use the **%UPCASE** function to redefine the value stored in the symbol table.

In situations where you intend to substitute the uppercased value many times, it is more efficient to redefine the variable than to execute the **%UPCASE** function repeatedly:

```
%let value=%upcase(&value);
```

Case of Text Issues

You can also transform text to lower or mixed case at the macro level.

Example: The MIXCASE macro creates a listing of all courses taught at a specified location (SITE parameter). The macro converts the supplied value of SITE to a text string beginning with a capital letter and followed by lowercased letters.

```
%macro mixcase(site);
   %let site=
      %upcase(%substr(&site,1,1))%lowcase(%substr(&site,2));
   proc print data=perm.schedule;
      where location="&site";
      title "Courses Offered in &site";
   run;
%mend;
```

The following macro calls all produce the same report.

```
%mixcase(dallas)
%mixcase(DALLAS)
%mixcase(daLLAs)
```

```
                    Courses Offered in Dallas

    OBS    CRSNUM    COURSE    LOCATION    BEGIN      TEACHER

     1       1       C001      Dallas     04FEB91    Hallis, Dr. George
     2       2       C002      Dallas     04MAR91    Wickam, Dr. Alice
     3       3       C003      Dallas     11MAR91    Forest, Mr. Peter
     4       4       C004      Dallas     25MAR91    Tally, Ms. Julia
     5       5       C005      Dallas     08APR91    Hallis, Dr. George
     6       6       C006      Dallas     06MAY91    Berthan, Ms. Judy
```

Note: %LOWCASE is not a macro function. It is a macro available in the AUTOCALL library supplied by SAS Institute. This is discussed in Chapter 6.

Case of Text Issues

General form of the **%SUBSTR** function:

%SUBSTR(*argument*, *position*, *n*)

The **%SUBSTR** function

- requires the first two arguments. The last argument is optional.

- returns the portion of *argument* beginning at *position* for a length of *n* characters.

- returns the portion of *argument* beginning at *position* to the end of *argument* when an *n* value is not supplied.

- produces a warning and reads from *position* to the end of *argument*, if an *n* value is supplied that extends beyond the bounds of *argument*.

You can specify *argument*, *position*, and *n* values using

- constant text

- macro variable references

- macro functions

- macro calls.

Note: The values of *position* and *n* can also be the result of an arithmetic expression. For example, `%substr(&var,%length(&var)-1)` returns the last two characters of the value of VAR.

Extracting Parts of Strings

You can assign several "words" to a macro variable's value and extract them with macro functions.

Example: Assign the value DALLAS 11MAR91 to SYSPARM. Create two macro variables SITE and DATE with values extracted from SYSPARM.

```
%let site=%scan(&sysparm,1);   =Dallas
%let date=%scan(&sysparm,2);   11MAR91
proc print data=perm.all noobs n;
   var name company cityst;
   where upcase(location)="&site";
   where also begin="&date"d;
   title "STUDENTS ENROLLED AT &site CENTER ON &date";
run;
```

Partial Listing

```
              STUDENTS ENROLLED AT DALLAS CENTER ON 11MAR91

   NAME                      COMPANY                     CITYST


   Bills, Ms. Paulette       Reston Railway              Chicago, IL
   Chevarley, Ms. Arlene     Motor Communications        Chicago, IL
   Clough, Ms. Patti         Reston Railway              Chicago, IL
   Crace, Mr. Ron            Von Crump Seafood           San Diego, CA
   Davis, Mr. Bruce          Semi;Conductor              Oakland, CA
```

Extracting Parts of Strings

General form of the %SCAN function:

   %SCAN(*argument, n, delimiters*)

The %SCAN function

* requires the first two arguments. The last argument is optional.

* returns the *n*th word of *argument*, where words are strings of characters separated by one or more delimiters.

* uses a default set of delimiters if none are specified.

* returns a null string if there are fewer than *n* words in *argument*.

You can specify values for *argument*, *n*, and *delimiters* using

* constant text

* macro variable references

* macro functions

* macro calls.

The default delimiters are:

   blank . < (+ | & ! $ *) ; ¬-/ , % \ >

Note: The value of *n* can also be an arithmetic expression.

   To use a blank as the only word delimiter, specify **%str( )** as the third argument. Use **%str(,)** to specify a comma delimiter.

Extracting Parts of Strings

You can test the value returned by the **%SCAN** function to find out how many "words" are in a character string.

Example: Assign one or two "words" to SYSPARM. Conditionally submit code based on the number of words supplied.

```
%macro students(values);
    %local site date;
    %let site=%scan(&values,1,#);
    %let date=%scan(&values,2,#);
    proc print data=perm.all noobs n;
        var name company cityst;
        where upcase(location)="&site";
        title "STUDENTS ENROLLED AT &site CENTER";
        %if &date ne %then %do;
            where also begin="&date"d;
            title2 "FOR COURSE STARTING &date";
        %end;
    run;
%mend;
```

Extracting Parts of Strings

If the value of SYSPARM is `SEATTLE#12AUG91`,

```
%students(&sysparm)
```

creates the report shown below.

Partial Listing

```
                    STUDENTS ENROLLED AT SEATTLE CENTER
                        FOR COURSE STARTING 12AUG91

    NAME                    COMPANY                     CITYST

    Blayney, Ms. Vivian     Southern Gas Co.            Los Angeles, CA
    Edwards, Mr. Charles    Gorman Tire Corp.           Akron, OH
    Ferraro, Mr. Mark       Quantum Corporation         Dallas, TX
```

If the value of SYSPARM is `BOSTON`,

```
%students(&sysparm)
```

creates the report shown below.

Partial Listing

```
                    STUDENTS ENROLLED AT BOSTON CENTER

    NAME                    COMPANY                     CITYST

    Allen, Ms. Denise       Department of Defense       Bethesda, MD
    Blayney, Ms. Vivian     Southern Gas Co.            Los Angeles, CA
    Brown, Mr. Michael      Swain Diagnostics Inc.      Columbia, MD
```

Searching for Words

A good technique when writing macros is to validate a macro variable's value before generating any SAS code based on this value.

Example: Create a report only if the value specified for the SITE parameter is DALLAS, SEATTLE, or BOSTON.

```
%macro courses(site);
    %let site=%upcase(&site);
    %if &site=DALLAS or &site=SEATTLE or &site=BOSTON %then
        %do;
        proc print data=perm.schedule;
            where upcase(location)="&site";
            title "COURSES OFFERED AT &site CENTER";
        run;
    %end;
%mend;
```

The macro call %courses(dallas) creates the report shown below.

```
                 COURSES OFFERED AT DALLAS CENTER

  OBS    CRSNUM    COURSE    LOCATION    BEGIN        TEACHER

   1        1       C001      Dallas     04FEB91    Hallis, Dr. George
   2        2       C002      Dallas     04MAR91    Wickam, Dr. Alice
   3        3       C003      Dallas     11MAR91    Forest, Mr. Peter
   4        4       C004      Dallas     25MAR91    Tally, Ms. Julia
   5        5       C005      Dallas     08APR91    Hallis, Dr. George
   6        6       C006      Dallas     06MAY91    Berthan, Ms. Judy
```

The macro call %courses(la) submits no SAS code.

Searching for Words

You can use the %INDEX function to simplify checking the value of a macro variable against a known list of values.

Example: Use the %INDEX function to validate the SITE parameter of the COURSES macro.

```
%macro courses(site);
   %local list;
   %let list=#DALLAS#SEATTLE#BOSTON#;
   %let site=%upcase(&site);
   %if %index(&list,#&site#)>0 %then %do;
      proc print data=perm.schedule;
         where upcase(location)="&site";
         title "COURSES OFFERED AT &site CENTER";
      run;
   %end;
%mend;
```

The # tokens serve to prevent unintentional pattern matches.

If you want to use blanks to separate the values, you must use a quoting function to preserve their meaning.

```
%let list=%str( DALLAS SEATTLE BOSTON );
%let site=%upcase(&site);
%if %index(&list,%str( &site ))>0 %then %do;
```

Searching for Words

General form of the **%INDEX** function:

%INDEX(*argument1*, *argument2*)

The **%INDEX** function

- searches the *argument1* string for the first occurrence of the string *argument2*

- returns a number representing the position in *argument1* of the first character of the *argument2* string when there is an exact pattern match

- returns 0 when there is no pattern match.

You can specify *argument1* and *argument2* values using

- constant text

- macro variable references

- macro functions

- macro calls.

Writing Text to the SAS Log

When errors or other irregularities occur in macro processing, you may want to write your own messages to the SAS log.

Example: Write a message to the SAS log if the value specified for the SITE parameter is not one of DALLAS, SEATTLE, or BOSTON.

```
%macro courses(site);
    %local list;
    %let list=%str( DALLAS SEATTLE BOSTON );
    %let site=%upcase(&site);
    %if %index(&list,%str( &site ))>0 %then %do;
        proc print data=perm.schedule;
            where upcase(location)="&site";
            title "COURSES OFFERED AT &site CENTER";
        run;
    %end;
    %else %do;
        %put;
        %put No courses taught at &site..;
        %put Use one of:&list;
        %put;
    %end;
%mend;
```

This macro call

```
%courses(la)
```

prints the following lines in the SAS log.

```
20          %courses(la)

No courses taught at LA.
Use one of: DALLAS SEATTLE BOSTON
```

Writing Text to the SAS Log

The **%PUT** statement writes text to the SAS log.

General form of the **%PUT** statement:

%PUT *text*;

The **%PUT** statement

- can be used inside or outside a macro definition.

- writes to the SAS log only.

- always writes to a new log line starting in column one. The statement **%PUT;** writes a blank line (line skip).

- removes leading and trailing blanks from *text* unless a macro quoting function is used. For example, **%put %str(text);**

- wraps lines when the length of *text* is greater than the current line size setting.

- resolves macro triggers in *text* before *text* is written.

- does not require quotes around *text*.

Creating a List of Data Values

You might want to validate a macro parameter's value against a list of all possible values that exist for a variable in a SAS data set.

Example: Suppose you do not know the names of all training sites, or the sites frequently change.

Write a generalized macro that creates a macro variable VALLIST that contains all unique values of a specified data set variable.

```
%macro values(dsn,var,delim=#);
   %let vallist=;
   proc sort data=&dsn(keep=&var) out=unique nodupkey;
      by &var;
   data _null_;
      set unique;
      call symput('vallist',
         symget('vallist')||"&delim"||trim(left(&var)));
   run;
   %let vallist=&vallist&delim;
%mend;
```

(handwritten annotations: Location (Boost Set Dall.) *; IS STORED IN ; (Symput) 'VALLIST' Line Above ; (# Boston))*

After calling the macro, you can check the value of the VALLIST variable.

```
%global vallist;
%values(perm.schedule,location)
%put Length of VALLIST is %length(&vallist);
%put;
%put &vallist;
```

Text Written to the SAS Log

```
Length of VALLIST is 23
#Boston#Dallas#Seattle#
```

(handwritten annotations: 1 2 3 over the text; → = VALLIST *)*

Creating a List of Data Values

The COURSES macro calls the VALUES macro to establish the value for
VALLIST.

```
%macro courses(site);
   %global vallist;
   %if &vallist= %then %values(perm.schedule,location);
   %let vallist=%upcase(&vallist);
   %let site=%upcase(&site);
   %if %index(&vallist,#&site#) gt 0 %then %do;
       proc print data=perm.schedule noobs;
           where upcase(location)="&site";
           title "COURSES OFFERED AT &site CENTER";
       run;
   %end;
   %else %put No courses taught at &site.;
%mend;
```

Don't need when to print
LA
delimiter   TEXT

```
%courses(dallas)
```

```
NOTE: The PROCEDURE PRINT printed page 1.
```

```
%courses(la)
```

```
No courses taught at LA.
```

How many times was the VALUES macro called after invoking COURSES twice?

Why was the VALLIST variable declared global instead of local?

Creating a List of Data Values

The following technique is valid when the length of the concatenated list of data values, including delimiters, does not exceed 200.

```
%global vallist;
%values(perm.students,cityst)
%put Length of VALLIST is %length(&vallist);
%put;
%put &vallist;
```

Text Written to the SAS Log

```
Length of VALLIST is 201

#Akron, OH#Albany, NY#Allentown, PA#Annapolis, MD#Atlanta,
GA#Austin, TX#Bethesda, MD#Birmingham, AL#Bozeman, MT#Brea,
CA#Buena Park, CA#Chicago, IL#Chicago, IN#Cincinati,
OH#Cleveland, OH#Columbia, M#
```

The SYMPUT routine can assign a maximum of 200 characters to VALLIST.

The SYMGET routine resolves only the first 200 characters of VALLIST.

Creating a List of Data Values

To avoid the 200 character limitation for the SYMPUT routine, you can execute a %LET statement under the control of the DATA step.

Example: Rewrite the VALUES macro so the VALLIST variable can hold all the values of a data set variable.

```
%macro values(dsn,var,delim=#);
   options nosource;
   %let vallist=;
   %local value;
   proc sort data=&dsn(keep=&var) out=unique nodupkey;
      by &var;
   data _null_;
      set unique;
      call symput('value',trim(left(&var)));
      call execute('%let vallist=&vallist&delim&value;');
   run;
   %let vallist=&vallist&delim;
   options source;
%mend;
```

After calling the macro, you can check the value of the VALLIST variable.

```
%global vallist;
%values(perm.students,cityst)
%put Length of VALLIST is %length(&vallist);
%put;
%put &vallist;
```

SAS Log Showing a Portion of the VALLIST Value

```
Length of VALLIST is 1045

#Akron, OH#Albany, NY#Allentown, PA#Annapolis, MD#Atlanta,
GA#Austin, TX#Bethesda, MD#Birmingham, AL#Bozeman, MT#Brea,
CA#Buena Park, CA#Chicago, IL#Chicago, IN#Cincinati,
OH#Cleveland, OH#Columbia, MD#Columbus, OH#Costa Mesa,
```

Creating a List of Data Values

The EXECUTE routine executes macro code during DATA step execution.

General form of the EXECUTE routine:

CALL EXECUTE(*expression*);

The value of *expression* can include

- global macro statements

- macro calls

- SAS statements.

Use single quotes around an *expression* containing macro triggers to prevent the macro processor from executing the expression during DATA step compilation.

Creating a List of Data Values

The SYMPUT routine and INTO clause store <u>any data value</u> in a macro variable.

Example: Create macro variables with the SYMPUT routine that contain
unquoted special characters. Demonstrate resolution problems.

```
data _null_;
   set problems;
   put _all_;
   call symput('val1',val1);
   call symput('val2',val2);
   call symput('val3',val3);
run;
```

Text Written to the SAS Log

```
VAL1=K&P Products VAL2=Semi;Conductor Corp. VAL3=Al's Diner
_ERROR_=0 _N_=1
```

Creating a List of Data Values

Resolving a macro variable that contains unquoted special characters can cause problems.

```
%put Resolving macro variables containing %str(&, ; and %');
%let p=alcan;
%put val1=*&val1*;
%put val2=*&val2*;
%put val3=*&val3*;
* more code;
* more code;
```

(2) Semicolons

Partial SAS Log

```
Resolving macro variables containing &, ; and '
SYMBOLGEN:  Macro variable VAL1 resolves to K&P Products
SYMBOLGEN:  Macro variable P resolves to alcan
val1=*Kalcan Products*
SYMBOLGEN:  Macro variable VAL2 resolves to Semi;Conductor Corp.
val2=*Semi
NOTE: Line generated by the macro variable "VAL2".
15          *Semi;Conductor Corp.
                     _____
                       180
ERROR 180-322: Statement is not valid or it is used out of
               proper order.


SYMBOLGEN:  Macro variable VAL3 resolves to Al's Diner
WARNING: The current word or quoted string has become more than
         200 characters long.  You may have unbalanced
         quotation marks.
val3=*Al's Diner*;
        * more code;
              * more code;
```

Creating a List of Data Values

The **%STR** function does not quote text resulting from macro variable resolution.

The **%SUPERQ** function is the most versatile of the several macro quoting functions that quote such text.

General form of the **%SUPERQ** function:

%SUPERQ(*macro-variable*)

macro-variable   is the name of an existing variable without a leading ampersand or an expression that reduces to the name of a macro variable.

Any tokens in the value of *macro-variable* that may need quoting are quoted.

Example: Use the **%SUPERQ** function to solve the resolution problems in the previous example.

```
%let p=alcan;
%put val1=*%superq(val1)*;
%put val2=*%superq(val2)*;
%put val3=*%superq(val3)*;
```

Text Written to the SAS Log

```
val1=*K&P Products*
val2=*Semi;Conductor Corp.*
val3=*Al's Diner*
```

Creating a List of Data Values

Example: Rewrite the VALUES macro so the VALLIST variable stores quoted
data values.

```
%macro values(dsn,var,delim=#);
   options nosource;
   %let vallist=;
   %local value;
   proc sort data=&dsn(keep=&var) out=unique nodupkey;
      by &var;
   data _null_;
      set unique;
      call symput('value',trim(left(&var)));
      call execute('%let vallist=
            &vallist&delim%superq(value);');
   run;
   %let vallist=&vallist&delim;
   options source;
%mend;
```

After calling the macro, you can check the value of the VALLIST variable.

```
%global vallist;
%values(perm.students,company)
%put Length of VALLIST is %length(&vallist);
%put;
%put &vallist;
```

SAS Log Showing a Portion of the VALLIST Value

```
Length of VALLIST is 2553

#Admiral Research & Development Co.#Al's Discount
Clothing#Alforone Chemical#Allied Wood Corporation#Amberly
Corp.#Animal Hospital#Applied Technologies#Assoc. of
Realtors#Atlantic Airways, Inc.#Autoloading Corp#ABC,
```

5.2 Iterative Processing

Simple Loops

Many macro applications require **iterative** processing.

With the iterative %DO statement you can repeatedly

- execute macro programming code

- generate SAS code.

Example: Demonstrate coding and execution of a simple iterative macro loop.

```
%macro doloop1;
    %local i;
    %do i=1 %to 4;
        %put index=&i;
    %end;
%mend;
%doloop1
```

Text Written to the SAS Log under the Control of the Loop

```
    index=1
    index=2
    index=3
    index=4
```

Simple Loops

General form of the iterative **%DO** statement:

> **%DO** *index-variable* = *start* **%TO** *stop* **%BY** *increment*; *(integer value only)*
>
> > *text*
>
> **%END**;

- The **%DO** and **%END** statements are valid only inside a macro definition.

- The *index-variable* is a macro variable.

- The *index-variable* is created if it does not already exist.

- The *start, stop*, and *increment* values can be any valid expressions that resolve to integers.

- The **%BY** clause is optional (default *increment* value is 1).

- The value of *text* can be

  — constant text

  — macro variables or expressions

  — macro statements

  — macro calls.

Simple Loops

Example: Demonstrate an iterative loop where macro variables initialize the start and stop values.

```
%macro doloop2(start,stop);
    options mprint;
    data _null_;
    %do i=&start %to &stop %by 2;
        val=&i;
        put val=roman.;
    %end;
    run;
%mend;
%doloop2(3,8)
```

The MPRINT option shows that multiple SAS statements are generated by the loop.

Text Written to the SAS Log

```
MPRINT(DOLOOP2):    DATA _NULL_;
MPRINT(DOLOOP2):    VAL=3;
MPRINT(DOLOOP2):    PUT VAL=ROMAN.;
MPRINT(DOLOOP2):    VAL=5;
MPRINT(DOLOOP2):    PUT VAL=ROMAN.;
MPRINT(DOLOOP2):    VAL=7;
MPRINT(DOLOOP2):    PUT VAL=ROMAN.;
MPRINT(DOLOOP2):    RUN;
```

When the DATA step executes, the following text is written to the SAS log.

```
VAL=III
VAL=V
VAL=VII
```

Simple Loops

Macro loops can generate complete SAS steps.

Example: Course offerings for several years are stored in a series of external files
that are identified by year. All the files have the same record layout.
Read each file into a separate SAS data set.

The READER macro creates one to three SAS data sets.

```
%macro reader(first=89,last=91);
    %if &first lt 89 or &last gt 91 %then
        %put No data available before 1989 or after 1991;
    %else %do;
        %local year;
        %do year=&first %to &last;
            filename in&year "edc.course&year..data";
            %if &sysfilrc ne 0 %then %str(endsas;);
        %end;
        %do year=&first %to &last;
            data year&year;
                infile in&year;
                input course $4. title $25. days 1. fee comma5.;
            run;
        %end;
    %end;
%mend;
```

Note: The SYSFILRC automatic variable is updated by a FILENAME
statement. It can be used to monitor the success of accessing an external
file.

The SYSLIBRC automatic variable is updated by the LIBNAME
statement. You can check it in a similar manner to monitor the success of
accessing a SAS data library.

Simple Loops

The following macro call generates three SAS data sets:

```
%reader()
```

Text Written to the SAS Log

```
MPRINT(READER):    FILENAME IN89 "edc.course89.data";
MPRINT(READER):    FILENAME IN90 "edc.course90.data";
MPRINT(READER):    FILENAME IN91 "edc.course91.data";
MPRINT(READER):    DATA YEAR89;
MPRINT(READER):    INFILE IN89;
MPRINT(READER):    INPUT COURSE $4. TITLE $25. DAYS 1. FEE COMMA5.;
MPRINT(READER):    RUN;

MPRINT(READER):    DATA YEAR90;
MPRINT(READER):    INFILE IN90;
MPRINT(READER):    INPUT COURSE $4. TITLE $25. DAYS 1. FEE COMMA5.;
MPRINT(READER):    RUN;

MPRINT(READER):    DATA YEAR91;
MPRINT(READER):    INFILE IN91;
MPRINT(READER):    INPUT COURSE $4. TITLE $25. DAYS 1. FEE COMMA5.;
MPRINT(READER):    RUN;
```

How would you create one data set for 1990?

Note: When a SAS step is submitted under the control of a macro, the macro
pauses its execution while the step executes. Control returns to the macro
after step execution.

Generating Data-dependent SAS Code

Example: The PERM.SCHEDULE data set contains schedule information for all
training locations. Create a separate data set for the schedule of each
individual location. You do not necessarily know how many locations
there are.

Partial Listing of the PERM.SCHEDULE Data Set

OBS	CRSNUM	COURSE	LOCATION (?)	BEGIN	TEACHER
1	1	C001	Dallas	04FEB91	Hallis, Dr. George
2	2	C002	Dallas	04MAR91	Wickam, Dr. Alice
3	3	C003	Dallas	11MAR91	Forest, Mr. Peter
4	4	C004	Dallas	25MAR91	Tally, Ms. Julia
5	5	C005	Dallas	08APR91	Hallis, Dr. George
6	6	C006	Dallas	06MAY91	Berthan, Ms. Judy
7	7	C001	Seattle	10JUN91	Hallis, Dr. George
8	8	C002	Seattle	17JUN91	Wickam, Dr. Alice
9	9	C003	Seattle	08JUL91	Forest, Mr. Peter
10	10	C004	Seattle	22JUL91	Tally, Ms. Julia
11	11	C005	Seattle	29JUL91	Tally, Ms. Julia
12	12	C006	Seattle	12AUG91	Berthan, Ms. Judy
13	13	C001	Boston	09SEP91	Hallis, Dr. George
14	14	C002	Boston	16SEP91	Wickam, Dr. Alice

SAS Log Showing Resulting Data Sets for Each Location

```
NOTE: The data set WORK.BOSTON has 6 observations and 5
      variables.
NOTE: The data set WORK.DALLAS has 6 observations and 5
      variables.
NOTE: The data set WORK.SEATTLE has 6 observations and 5
      variables.
```

Generating Data-dependent SAS Code

The macro language does not support variable lists or array structures. However, you can use iterative macro loops to create or process a series of related macro variables.

Example: Use the DATA step to create a series of macro variables, one for each different site where courses are taught and a macro loop to display the created macro variables.

```
%macro sites;
   proc sort data=perm.schedule out=values nodupkey;
      by location;
   data _null_;
      set values end=last;
      call symput('site'||left(_n_),trim(upcase(location)));
      if last then call symput('total',left(_n_));
   run;
   %do i=1 %to &total;
      %put site&i => &&site&i;
   %end;
%mend;

%sites
```

Text Written to the SAS Log

```
site1 => BOSTON
site2 => DALLAS
site3 => SEATTLE
TOTAL = 3
```

Note: The SITE variables are created in the global symbol table because no local table is created by the SITES macro.

Generating Data-dependent SAS Code

Example: Add code to the SITES macro that will generate a DATA step to create
a separate data set for each distinct value of LOCATION.

```
%macro sites;
    proc sort data=perm.schedule out=values nodupkey;
       by location;
    data _null_;
       set values end=last;
       call symput('site'||left(_n_),trim(upcase(location)));
       if last then call symput('total',left(_n_));
    run;

    %local i;
    data
    %do i=1 %to &total;
       &&site&i
    %end;
       set perm.schedule;
       select (upcase(location));
          %do i=1 %to &total;
             when ("&&site&i") output &&site&i;
          %end;
             otherwise;
       end;
    run;
%mend;

%sites
```

Handwritten annotations:

DATA-STATEMENT
BOSTON?
'3X' Creating
(Data Steps)
3
DATA BOSTON DALLAS SEATTLE j
SET. PERM. schedule

Generating Data-dependent SAS Code

Partial SAS Log with the MPRINT System Option in Effect

```
MPRINT(SITES):    PROC SORT DATA=PERM.SCHEDULE OUT=VALUES
NODUPKEY;
MPRINT(SITES):    BY LOCATION;

NOTE: 15 observations with duplicate key values were deleted.
NOTE: The data set WORK.VALUES has 3 observations and 5
      variables.

MPRINT(SITES):    DATA _NULL_;
MPRINT(SITES):    SET VALUES END=LAST;
MPRINT(SITES):    CALL
SYMPUT('site'||LEFT(_N_),TRIM(UPCASE(LOCATION)));
MPRINT(SITES):    IF LAST THEN CALL SYMPUT('total',LEFT(_N_));
MPRINT(SITES):    RUN;

MPRINT(SITES):    DATA BOSTON DALLAS SEATTLE ;
MPRINT(SITES):    SET PERM.SCHEDULE;
MPRINT(SITES):    SELECT (UPCASE(LOCATION));
MPRINT(SITES):    WHEN ("BOSTON") OUTPUT BOSTON;
MPRINT(SITES):    WHEN ("DALLAS") OUTPUT DALLAS;
MPRINT(SITES):    WHEN ("SEATTLE") OUTPUT SEATTLE;
MPRINT(SITES):    OTHERWISE;
MPRINT(SITES):    END;
MPRINT(SITES):    RUN;
```

5.3 Arithmetic and Logical Operations

The %EVAL Function

The SAS macro language allows the evaluation of logical and arithmetic expressions through a special function named %EVAL.

General form of the %EVAL function:

%EVAL(*expression*)

The %EVAL function

- translates integer strings (such as **235**) and hexadecimal strings (such as **3fax**) to integers. The largest representable integer is 2147483647.

- translates tokens representing arithmetic, comparison, and logical operators to macro-level operators.

- performs arithmetic and logical operations.

- truncates the result of an arithmetic operation that produces a noninteger to an integer.

- returns the result of an arithmetic operation as a character string.

- returns 1 (true) or 0 (false) for logical operations.

- returns a null value and issues an error message when noninteger values are used in arithmetic operations.

Note: The **%EVAL** function does not convert the following to numeric values:

  - numeric strings containing a period or E-notation

  - SAS date and time constants.

The %EVAL Function

The tokens shown in the two leftmost columns have arithmetic or logical meaning to the **%EVAL** function.

Operator	Mnemonic	Meaning	Precedence
**		exponentiation	1
¬	NOT	logical not	1
*		multiplication	2
/		division	2
+		addition	3
-		subtraction	3
<	LT	less than	4
< =	LE	less than or equal	4
=	EQ	equal	4
¬ =	NE	not equal	4
>	GT	greater than	4
> =	GE	greater than or equal	4
&	AND	logical and	5
|	OR	logical or	6

Note: As in the DATA step, parentheses can be used to control the order of operations.

The %EVAL Function

Example: Use the **%EVAL** function to evaluate various expressions.

These statements	Generate these results
`%put value=%eval(10 lt 2);`	`value=0`
`%put value=10+2;`	`value=10+2`
`%put value=%eval(10+2);`	`value=12`

`%let counter=2;`
`%let counter=%eval(&counter+1);`
`%put counter=&counter;`
	`counter=3`

`%let numer=2;`
`%let denom=8;`
`%put value=%eval(&numer/&denom);`
	`value=0`

`%let real=2.4;`
`%let int=8;`
`%put value=%eval(&real+&int);`
	`value=`

In the last example, the **%EVAL** function creates an error condition and returns a null value. The message written to the SAS log is shown below.

```
ERROR: A character operand was found in the %EVAL function or
       %IF condition where a numeric operand is required. The
       condition was: 2.4+8
```

Conditional Loops

You can perform conditional iteration in macros with **%DO %WHILE** and **%DO %UNTIL** statements.

General form of the **%DO %WHILE** statement:

> **%DO %WHILE**(*expression*);
>
>> *text*
>
> **%END**;

General form of the **%DO %UNTIL** statement:

> **%DO %UNTIL**(*expression*);
>
>> *text*
>
> **%END**;

expression   can be any valid macro expression.

A **%DO %WHILE** loop

- evaluates *expression* at the top of the loop before the loop executes

- executes repetitively while *expression* is true.

A **%DO %UNTIL** loop

- evaluates *expression* at the bottom of the loop after the loop executes

- executes repetitively until *expression* is true

- executes at least once.

Conditional Loops

The SAFELOOP macro demonstrates how you can terminate a conditional loop after a fixed number of iterations if the WHILE or UNTIL condition does not terminate the loop.

```
%macro safeloop(val,maxloop=100);
   %local i;

   %let i=0;
   %do %until(&val or &i=&maxloop);
      %* macro coding affecting value of &val;
      %let i=%eval(&i+1);
   %end;
   %put UNTIL loop executions=&i;

   %let i=0;
   %do %while(not(&val) and &i<&maxloop);
      %* macro coding affecting value of &val;
      %let i=%eval(&i+1);
   %end;
   %put WHILE loop executions=&i;
%mend;
%safeloop(1)
```

Text Written to the SAS Log

```
UNTIL loop executions=1
WHILE loop executions=0
```

```
%safeloop(0)
```

Text Written to the SAS Log

```
UNTIL loop executions=100
WHILE loop executions=100
```

5.4 More about %EVAL and Macro Quoting (Optional)

Introduction

If you understand the basic concepts and syntax of the macro language presented so far, you can write most applications without problems.

As you gain more experience with the macro language and attempt to write more complex applications, you may encounter problems with

- logical comparisons of integers and character strings

- where you can use arithmetic expressions in macro coding

- tokens being interpreted as macro syntax when you do not want them to be

- tokens that lose their quoting after being manipulated by a macro function

- tokens that need to be quoted indirectly.

These programming issues are explored in this section.

Automatic Evaluation

Any macro language function or statement that requires a numeric or logical expression automatically invokes the **%EVAL** function:

%SCAN(*text*,**expression**,*delimiters*)

%SUBSTR(*text*,**expression**,**expression**)

%IF **expression** %THEN *text*;

%DO *index* = **expression** %TO **expression**
    %BY **expression**;

%DO %UNTIL(**expression**);

%DO %WHILE(**expression**);

The following **%SUBSTR** functions generate the same result:

```
%substr(&var,%length(&var)-1)

%substr(&var,%eval(%length(&var)-1))
```

The second example is less efficient because the **%EVAL** function is invoked twice:

1.   explicitly by the **%EVAL** function

2.   implicitly by the **%SUBSTR** function.

Compilation versus Execution of Expressions

The macro shown below contains an invalid operator in the second **%IF** expression. Because the macro processor does not evaluate expressions during compilation, the macro compiles successfully.

```
%macro compare(x,y);
    %if &x gt &y %then %put &x is greater than &y;
    %else %if &x ls &y %then %put &x is less than &y;
    %else %put &x equals &y;
%mend;
```

The following macro call does not generate an error because the second **%IF** expression is not executed.

```
%compare(100,5)
```

Text Written to the SAS Log

```
100 is greater than 5
```

The following macro call does generate an error because the second **%IF** expression is executed.

```
%compare(5,100)
```

Partial SAS Log

```
ERROR: A character operand was found in the %EVAL function or
       %IF condition where a numeric operand is required. The
       condition was: &x ls &y
ERROR: The macro will stop executing.
```

Comparisons Using the %EVAL Function

Rules for comparison operations within the **%EVAL** function:

1. If two integers are compared, arithmetic comparison is used.

2. If a character string is compared to an integer, or two character strings are compared, character comparison is used.

The expression

```
%eval(5 gt 100)
```

returns 0 (false).

The expression

```
%eval(5.0 gt 100)
```

returns 1 (true) because **5.0** is not an integer.

Character comparison is used:

```
operand1   5.0
             =

operand2   100
             =
```

In a collating sequence, 5 is greater than 1. Therefore, the character string **5.0** is greater than **100**.

Likewise, the expression

```
%eval(5.00 gt 5.0)
```

returns 1 (true) because the fourth character of **5.00** compares greater than the blank padded to **5.0** as the fourth character.

Comparisons Using the %EVAL Function

Additional Rules for Using the **%EVAL** Function:

1.   Arithmetic and comparison expressions must be "balanced":

     %eval(*operand operator operand*)

2.   All tokens in an expression have arithmetic, logical, or other syntactic meaning, unless their meaning is removed.

The following comparison causes an error

```
%eval(OR gt OK)
```

because **OR** is treated as an operator and creates an unbalanced expression.

You can remove the meaning of special tokens by using a macro quoting function:

```
%eval(%str(OR) gt OK)
```

returns 1 (true).

Problems with Comparisons

The **%STR** function

- performs its quoting as it is encountered (at compilation)

- quotes the constant text that appears in its argument

- permits macro resolution within its argument

- does not quote text that results from macro resolution.

Example: Attempt to quote values that are supplied during macro execution.

```
%macro compare(x,y);
    %if %str(&x)=%str(&y) %then %put &x = &y;
    %else %put &x not equal to &y;
%mend;

%compare(+,-)
```

SAS Log Showing Execution Errors

```
ERROR: A character operand was found in the %EVAL function or
       %IF condition where a numeric operand is required. The
       condition was: &x=&y
ERROR: The macro will stop executing.
```

The **%STR** function performed its quoting during macro compilation.

During macro execution, the unbalanced expression + = - caused the error.

Problems with Comparisons

To solve this problem, you can use the **%SUPERQ** quoting function.

The **%SUPERQ** function

- uses a single macro variable as it argument (no &)

- quotes all text in the value of its argument: special characters, operators, unmatched quotes or parentheses, and macro triggers

- performs its quoting during macro execution.

Example: Quote values that are supplied during macro execution.

```
%macro compare(x,y);
   %if %superq(x)=%superq(y) %then %put &x = &y;
   %else %put &x not equal to &y;
%mend;

%compare(+,-)
%compare(LT,LE)
%compare(NOT,NOT)
%compare(&,=)
```

SAS Log Showing Macro Execution Results

```
+ not equal to -
LT not equal to LE
NOT = NOT
& not equal to =
```

Problems with Comparisons

Another type of quoting problem can arise when you extract strings with the **%SUBSTR** or **%SCAN** function or translate strings with the **%UPCASE** function.

Example: Attempt to compare values resulting from a **%SUBSTR** function.

```
%macro find(x,y);
   %if %substr(&x,1,%length(&y))=%superq(y) %then
      %put &x starts with &y;
   %else %put &x does not start with &y;
%mend;

%find(OREGON,OR)
```

SAS Log Showing Macro Execution Results

```
ERROR: A character operand was found in the %EVAL function or
       %IF condition where a numeric operand is required. The
       condition was: %substr(&x,1,%length(&y))=%superq(y)
ERROR: The macro will stop executing.
```

The text OR returned by the **%SUBSTR** function is interpreted as a logical operator.

Problems with Comparisons

The **%QSUBSTR**, **%QSCAN**, and **%QUPCASE** functions quote (or preserve quoting in) the returned value.

Example: Use the **%QSUBSTR** function to quote its result.

```
%macro find(x,y);
   %if %qsubstr(&x,1,%length(&y))=%superq(y) %then
      %put &x starts with &y;
   %else %put &x does not start with &y;
%mend;

%find(OREGON,OR)
%find(+23,-)
%find("TEXT",%str(%"))
```

SAS Log Showing Macro Execution Results

```
OREGON starts with OR
+23 does not start with -
"TEXT" starts with "
```

5.5 Exercises

5.1   Validating Macro Parameters

a.   Include the program C5EX1 shown below into the PROGRAM EDITOR window and submit it.

```
%macro paid(crsnum);
    title "Fee Status for Course &crsnum";
    proc print data=perm.register label n noobs;
       var name paid;
       where crsnum=&crsnum;
    run;
%mend;

%paid(2)
```

b.   Recall the macro and modify it so it conditionally submits the PROC PRINT step only if the CRSNUM parameter has a value between 1 and 18. If the CRSNUM value is out of range, the macro should write the following messages to the SAS log:

```
Course Number must be between 1 and 18
Supplied value was:  x
```

The value of x is the CRSNUM parameter.

Resubmit the macro definition and call the macro using both valid and invalid parameter values.

c.   Recall the macro definition and supply a second positional parameter named STATUS. Alter the PAID macro so that it submits the following statement immediately after the WHERE statement, providing STATUS has a valid value of **Y** or **N**

```
where also paid="&status";
```

Resubmit the macro definition and call the macro using both valid and invalid values for STATUS.

Exercises

5.1   Validating Macro Parameters (continued)

d.   Recall the macro definition and alter it so that it will accept any word beginning with **Y** or **N** in any case as a value for STATUS. The macro should alter the value of STATUS so that only the first character, in uppercase, is stored. Call the macro several times using the following code:

```
%paid(2,no)
%paid(2,y)
%paid(2)
```

5.2   Using Macro Functions

a.   Include the program C5EX2 shown below into the PROGRAM EDITOR window and submit it. This program uses a PROC SQL dictionary table to display the variables in a specified data set.

```
title "Variables in PERM.SCHEDULE";
proc sql;
    select name, type, length
        from dictionary.columns
        where libname="PERM" and
                memname="SCHEDULE";
quit;
```

b.   Recall the program and alter it so that the code is part of a macro named FINDVAR. Change the code so that the macro displays a report of the variables from the most recently created data set. The name of this data set can be found through the SYSLAST macro variable. You will need to use one or more macro functions to separate the value of SYSLAST into the library reference and the data set name.

Use a %LET statement to set the value of the SYSLAST macro variable to PERM.SCHEDULE. Call the FINDVAR macro.

c.   Use a %LET statement to set the value of the SYSLAST macro variable to PERM.COURSES. Call the FINDVAR macro.

Exercises

5.3   Using Macro DO Loops (Optional)

Include the program C5EX3 shown below into the PROGRAM EDITOR window. This program uses a SASHELP dictionary view to create a separate macro variable (DSNAME1, DSNAME2, and so on) for each data set in the PERM library. The macro variable TOTALDSN is created containing the total number of data sets in the library.

```
data _null_;
   set sashelp.vstabvw end=final;
   where libname="PERM";
   call symput('dsname'||trim(left(_n_)),trim(memname));
   if final then call symput('totaldsn',trim(left(_n_)));
run;
```

Use the above code as part of a macro which will generate a PROC PRINT step for each data set in a specified library. The macro should have two parameters:

LIBREF   is the positional parameter specifying the library.

NOBS   is the keyword parameter indicating the number of observations to be output by each PROC PRINT step (default value = 5).

(Hint: As you modify the WHERE statement in the DATA step to accept the LIBREF macro variable, be aware that library names in the SASHELP views are in uppercase.)

5.6 Chapter Summary

Many applications require manipulation of macro variable values such as extracting a portion of the value, translating text to uppercase, and so on. The macro language provides basic character string functions that are similar to their DATA step counterparts (for example, the **%SUBSTR**, **%SCAN**, and **%UPCASE** functions).

The macro processor automatically performs logical operations and integer arithmetic within **%IF** expressions, **%DO** loops, and certain functions. You can explicitly request integer arithmetic and logical evaluation operations with the **%EVAL** function.

The **%PUT** statement is used to write your own text to the SAS log. This is helpful when you want to print out the value of a macro variable or conditionally write notes to the SAS log during macro execution. These notes may explain irregular situations or issue confirmation messages.

A very useful macro programming technique is to create a series of macro variables to store a related set of values (such as an array). Another technique stores many values in one macro variable and uses **%DO** loops and macro functions to extract the values. These techniques enable you to write programs that perform table lookup operations and validation tasks.

Whenever a macro variable is assigned a value by a DATA step, PROC SQL, or other indirect means such as a macro window or the SYSPARM variable, there is a possibility that resolving the variable may produce unexpected results. This happens when the value contains special characters such as a semicolon, a macro trigger (R&D, for example), or unmatched quotes (CAN'T, for example). To avoid such resolution problems, you should use a macro quoting function such as **%SUPERQ** to remove the meaning of special characters during macro execution. Remember that the **%STR** function only quotes characters that openly appear in its argument, not characters that result from macro resolution within its argument.

Other character functions such as **%UPCASE**, **%SCAN**, and **%SUBSTR** have counterparts **%QUPCASE**, **%QSCAN**, and **%QSUBSTR** that cause the returned value to be (or remain) quoted. See the PROCESS macro in Appendix A for additional applications of these quoting functions.

Chapter Summary

Macro character functions:

%SUBSTR(*argument, position, n*)

%SCAN(*argument, n, delimiters*)

%INDEX(*argument1, argument2*)

General form of the **%PUT** statement:

%PUT *text*;

General form of the EXECUTE routine:

CALL EXECUTE(*'expression'*);

Selected macro quoting function:

%SUPERQ(*macro-variable*)

General form of the iterative **%DO** statement:

%DO *index-variable* = *start* **%TO** *stop* **%BY** *increment*;

   text

%END;

General form of the **%EVAL** function:

%EVAL(*expression*)

Chapter Summary

General form of the **%DO %WHILE** statement:

%DO %WHILE(*expression*);

   text

%END;

General form of the **%DO %UNTIL** statement:

%DO %UNTIL(*expression*);

   text

%END;

5.7 Solutions and Selected Output

5.1   Validating Macro Parameters

b.

```
%macro paid(crsnum);
    %if &crsnum ge 1 and &crsnum le 18 %then %do;
        title "Fee Status for Course &crsnum";
        proc print data=perm.register label n noobs;
            var name paid;
            where crsnum=&crsnum;
        run;
    %end;
    %else %do;
        %put Course Number must be between 1 and 18;
        %put Supplied value was: &crsnum;
    %end;
%mend;
%paid(20)
```

Partial SAS Log

```
Course Number must be between 1 and 18
Supplied value was: 20
```

Solutions and Selected Output

5.1   Validating Macro Parameters (continued)

c.

```
%macro paid(crsnum,status);
    %if &crsnum gt 1 and &crsnum le 18 %then %do;
        title "Fee Status for Course &crsnum";
        proc print data=perm.register label n noobs;
            var name paid;
            where crsnum=&crsnum;
        %if %index(YN,&status)>0 %then %do;
            where also paid="&status";
        %end;
        run;
    %end;
    %else %do;
        %put Course Number must be between 1 and 18;
        %put Supplied value was: &crsnum;
    %end;
%mend;
```

d.

```
%macro paid(crsnum,status);
    %if &crsnum gt 1 and &crsnum le 18 %then %do;
        title "Fee Status for Course &crsnum";
        proc print data=perm.register label n noobs;
            var name paid;
            where crsnum=&crsnum;
        %let status=%substr(%upcase(&status),1,1);
        %if %index(YN,&status)>0 %then %do;
            where also paid="&status";
        %end;
        run;
    %end;
    %else %do;
        %put Course Number must be between 1 and 18;
        %put Supplied value was: &crsnum;
    %end;
%mend;
```

Solutions and Selected Output

5.1   Validating Macro Parameters (continued)

d.   (continued)

```
%paid(2,no)
```

Partial Output

```
              Fee Status for Course 2

                                   Paid
          Student Name             Status

          Divjak, Ms. Theresa        N
          Gandy, Dr. David           N
          Harrell, Mr. Ken           N
```

```
%paid(2,y)
```

Partial Output

```
              Fee Status for Course 2

                                   Paid
          Student Name             Status

          Amigo, Mr. Bill            Y
          Benincasa, Ms. Elizabeth   Y
          Brown, Mr. Michael         Y
```

Solutions and Selected Output

5.1   Validating Macro Parameters (continued)

d.   (continued)

```
%paid(2)
```

Partial Output

```
                    Fee Status for Course 2

                                          Paid
            Student Name                  Status

            Amigo, Mr. Bill                 Y
            Benincasa, Ms. Elizabeth        Y
            Brown, Mr. Michael              Y
            Divjak, Ms. Theresa             N
```

Solutions and Selected Output

5.2   Using Macro Functions

b.

```
%macro findvar;
    %let lib=%scan(&syslast,1,.);
    %let dsn=%scan(&syslast,2,.);
    title "Variables in &syslast";
    proc sql;
        select name, type, length
            from dictionary.columns
            where libname="&lib" and
                    memname="&dsn";
    quit;
%mend findvar;
%let syslast=PERM.SCHEDULE;
%findvar
```

Alternate Solution

```
%macro findvar;
    %let period=%index(&syslast,.);
    %let lib=%substr(&syslast,1,%eval(&period-1));
    %let dsn=%substr(&syslast,%eval(&period+1));
    title "Variables in &syslast";
    proc sql;
        select name, type, length
            from dictionary.columns
            where libname="&lib" and
                    memname="&dsn";
    quit;
%mend findvar;
```

Solutions and Selected Output

5.2   Using Macro Functions (continued)

b.   (continued)

```
              Variables in PERM.SCHEDULE

              Column    Column    Column
              Name      Type      Length
              -------------------------------
              CRSNUM    num            8
              COURSE    char           4
              LOCATION  char          15
              BEGIN     num            8
              TEACHER   char          20
```

c.

```
    %let syslast=PERM.COURSES;
    %findvar
```

```
              Variables in PERM.COURSES

              Column    Column    Column
              Name      Type      Length
              -------------------------------
              COURSE    char           4
              TITLE     char          25
              DAYS      num            8
              FEE       num            8
```

Solutions and Selected Output

5.3   Using Macro DO Loops (Optional)

```
%macro document(libref,nobs=5);
   data _null_;
      set sashelp.vstabvw end=final;
      where libname="%upcase(&libref)";
      call symput('dsname'||trim(left(_n_)),
           trim(memname));
      if final then call symput('totaldsn',
         trim(left(_n_)));
   run;
   %local i;
   %do i=1 %to &totaldsn;
      proc print data=&libref..&&dsname&i(obs=&nobs);
      options pageno=1 date;
      title "Listing of %upcase(&libref).&&dsname&i";
      run;
   %end;
%mend;
%document(perm)
```

Solutions and Selected Output

5.3   Using Macro DO Loops (Optional) (continued)

Partial SAS Log with MPRINT System Option in Effect

```
MPRINT(DOCUMENT):    PROC PRINT DATA=PERM.ALL(OBS=5);
MPRINT(DOCUMENT):    OPTIONS PAGENO=1 DATE;
MPRINT(DOCUMENT):    TITLE "Listing of PERM.ALL";
MPRINT(DOCUMENT):    RUN;

MPRINT(DOCUMENT):    PROC PRINT DATA=PERM.COURSES(OBS=5);
MPRINT(DOCUMENT):    OPTIONS PAGENO=1 DATE;
MPRINT(DOCUMENT):    TITLE "Listing of PERM.COURSES";
MPRINT(DOCUMENT):    RUN;

MPRINT(DOCUMENT):    PROC PRINT DATA=PERM.REGISTER(OBS=5);
MPRINT(DOCUMENT):    OPTIONS PAGENO=1 DATE;
MPRINT(DOCUMENT):    TITLE "Listing of PERM.REGISTER";
MPRINT(DOCUMENT):    RUN;

MPRINT(DOCUMENT):    PROC PRINT DATA=PERM.SCHEDULE(OBS=5);
MPRINT(DOCUMENT):    OPTIONS PAGENO=1 DATE;
MPRINT(DOCUMENT):    TITLE "Listing of PERM.SCHEDULE";
MPRINT(DOCUMENT):    RUN;

MPRINT(DOCUMENT):    PROC PRINT DATA=PERM.STUDENTS(OBS=5);
MPRINT(DOCUMENT):    OPTIONS PAGENO=1 DATE;
MPRINT(DOCUMENT):    TITLE "Listing of PERM.STUDENTS";
MPRINT(DOCUMENT):    RUN;
```

6. Macro Efficiencies

Version
6.06

6.1 The Autocall Facility

6.2 The Stored Compiled Macro Facility

6.3 Memory Management (Optional)

6.4 Efficient Macro Programming (Optional)

6.5 Chapter Summary

6.1 The Autocall Facility

Making Macros Available to Your Session

There are four basic ways of making macros accessible to your SAS session or job:

- Submit all macro definitions in the program before calling them.

- Use **%INCLUDE** statements to submit macro definitions stored in external files.

- Use the *autocall facility* to search predefined source libraries for macro definitions.

- Access permanent SAS catalogs that contain compiled macros.

Advantages to using the autocall facility are:

- You do not have to submit the source code for the macro definition before calling the macro.

- Conditionally executed macros are compiled only if they are actually invoked.

- Multiple autocall libraries can be set up.

Using the Autocall Facility *% footnote*

To use the autocall facility,

1. create a *source library* on your operating system for macro definitions:

    MVS   partitioned data set (PDS)

    CMS   a file of file type MACLIB

    VMS   directory with source files (filetype .SAS) or a VMS text
                   library (filetype .TLB)

2. place each macro definition in a separate member (file) of the source library.
    The macro name and the member name must be the same.

3. use the SAS system option SASAUTOS= to identify the name of the
    autocall library or associate a fileref of SASAUTOS with the autocall library.

4. specify the SAS system option MAUTOSOURCE. *on*

5. call any macro in the library during the SAS session.

Note: SAS Institute provides an autocall library with the SAS System. In most
        cases, it is desirable to concatenate your autocall libraries with the autocall
        library supplied by SAS Institute.

        Releases 6.03 and 6.04 of the SAS System do not support the autocall
        facility.

Using the Autocall Facility

With the autocall facility in effect, invoking a macro that is not previously defined causes the macro facility to

- search the autocall library for a member with the same name as the macro being invoked

- bring the source statements into the current SAS session if the member is found

- issue an error message if the member is not found

- submit all statements in the member to define the macro

- call the macro.

The autocall facility does not search for a macro in the autocall library if the macro is already defined in the current SAS session.

The MAUTOSOURCE and SASAUTOS = Options

The MAUTOSOURCE system option controls whether the autocall facility is available:

OPTIONS MAUTOSOURCE;

OPTIONS NOMAUTOSOURCE;

The MAUTOSOURCE system option is the default.

The SASAUTOS = system option controls where the macro facility looks for autocall macros:

OPTIONS SASAUTOS = *library1*;

OPTIONS SASAUTOS = (*library1*, . . . , *libraryn*);

The values of *library1* through *libraryn* are references to source libraries containing macro definitions. You specify a source library by either

- placing its name in quotes, or

- pointing to it with a fileref.

The default is SASAUTOS = SASAUTOS.

Note: The reserved fileref SASAUTOS is assigned to the default autocall library at invocation time. This may be a library supplied by the SAS Institute or another designated by your site.

The MAUTOSOURCE and SASAUTOS = system options can be set at SAS invocation or with an OPTIONS statement during program execution.

Using the Autocall Facility in MVS Batch

In an MVS batch environment, a

- user autocall library is created by placing each macro definition in a separate member of a partitioned data set (*member-name* = *macro-name*)

- JCL DD statement is used to allocate autocall libraries with a DDname of SASAUTOS.

The following JCL illustrates how to specify a single user autocall library:

```
//MYJOB     JOB  account, . . .
//          EXEC SAS6,OPTIONS='MAUTOSOURCE'
//SASAUTOS  DD   DSN=MY.MACROS,DISP=SHR
```

The following JCL illustrates how to concatenate user autocall libraries ahead of the default autocall library.

```
//MYJOB     JOB  account, . . .
//          EXEC SAS6,OPTIONS='MAUTOSOURCE'
//SASAUTOS  DD   DSN=MY.MACROS1,DISP=SHR
//          DD   DSN=MY.MACROS2,DISP=SHR
//          DD   DSN=default.autocall.library,DISP=SHR
```

Note: The libraries are searched in the order they are concatenated.

You can find the name of the default autocall library in the JCL printout from any SAS job.

Using the Autocall Facility in TSO

In a TSO environment,

- a user autocall library is created by placing each macro definition in a separate member of a partitioned data set (*member name = macro name*)

- the OPTIONS operand of the SAS Institute-supplied CLIST is used to specify system options at SAS invocation.

You want a single autocall library searched:

[handwritten: Goto Display Manager]

```
sas6 options('mautosource sasautos="tsoid.macros"')
      input('''program-name''')
```

[handwritten: Parameter in CList)]

You want multiple libraries searched:

```
sas6 options('mautosource
      sasautos=("tsoid.macros1","tsoid.macros2",sasautos)')
      input('''program-name''')
```

The SASAUTOS fileref (DDname) points to the default autocall library. It is automatically allocated by the SAS System.

You can omit the INPUT CLIST operand if you want to start an interactive session with the autocall facility in effect.

Using the Autocall Facility in TSO

Instead of specifying the MAUTOSOURCE and SASAUTOS= system options at job invocation, you can use an OPTIONS statement at the beginning of a SAS program executed under MVS batch or TSO.

You want a single autocall library searched:

```
options mautosource sasautos='tsoid.macros';
```

You want multiple libraries searched:

```
options mautosource
        sasautos=('tsoid.macros1','tsoid.macros2',sasautos);
```

Using the Autocall Facility in CMS

In a CMS environment,

- a user autocall library is created by placing each macro definition in a separate member of a file with a file type of MACLIB

- you specify invocation options following a parenthesis in the SAS command.

You can specify a single autocall library at job invocation:

```
sas6 program-name (mautosource sasautos='my maclib a'
```

You can specify multiple libraries at job invocation:

```
sas6 program-name (mautosource
      sasautos=('my1 maclib a','my2 maclib a',sasautos)
```

Instead, you could include an OPTIONS statement in your program:

```
options mautosource sasautos='my maclib a';

options mautosource
      sasautos=('my1 maclib a','my2 maclib a',sasautos);
```

Using the Autocall Facility in VMS

In a VMS environment,

- a user autocall library is created by placing each macro definition in a separate file (filetype .SAS) of a directory or in separate members of a VMS text library (filetype .TLB)

- invocation options are separated by slashes following the SAS command.

You can specify a single autocall library at SAS invocation:

```
sas6/mautosource/sasautos='[mydir]' [dir]program
```

You can specify multiple libraries at SAS invocation:

```
sas6/mautosource/sasautos=('[mydir1]','[mydir2]',sasautos)
    [dir]program
```

You can also use an OPTIONS statement in your program:

```
options mautosource sasautos='[mydir]';

options mautosource
        sasautos=('[mydir1]','[mydir2]',sasautos);
```

Institute-Supplied Autocall Library

SAS Institute provides several macros in an autocall library that is supplied with the installation tape. Your site may include these macros in the default autocall library.

Selected macros in the autocall library:

%LOWCASE(*argument*)

converts letters in its argument from uppercase to lowercase.

%QLOWCASE(*argument*)

converts letters in its argument from uppercase to lowercase and quotes the returned string.

%LEFT(*argument*)   removes the leading blanks from the argument.

%TRIM(*argument*)   trims trailing blanks from the argument.

%CMPRES(*argument*)

removes multiple blanks from the argument.

%DATATYP(*argument*)

returns the string NUMERIC or CHAR, depending on whether the argument is an integer or a character string.

The %LOWCASE Macro

The macro definition for the **%LOWCASE** macro is shown below.

```
%macro lowcase(string);
%****************************************************************;
%*                                                              *;
%*    MACRO: LOWCASE                                            *;
%*                                                              *;
%*    USAGE: %lowcase(argument)                                 *;
%*                                                              *;
%*    DESCRIPTION:                                              *;
%*       This macro returns the argument passed to it           *;
%*       unchanged except that all uppercase alphabetic         *;
%*       characters are changed to lowercase equivalents.       *;
%*                                                              *;
%*    NOTES:                                                    *;
%*       Although the argument to the %UPCASE function may      *;
%*       contain commas, the argument to %LOWCASE may not,      *;
%*       unless they are quoted. Because %LOWCASE is a macro*;
%*       it interprets a comma as the end of a parameter.       *;
%*                                                              *;
%****************************************************************;

%local i c index result;
%do i=1 %to %length(&string);
   %let c=%substr(&string,&i,1);
   %if &c eq %then %let c=%str( );
   %else %do;
      %let index=%index(ABCDEFGHIJKLMNOPQRSTUVWXYZ,&c);
      %if &index gt 0 %then
         %let c=%substr(abcdefghijklmnopqrstuvwxyz,&index,1);
      %end;
   %let result=&result.&c;
   %end;
&result
%mend;
```

6.2 The Stored Compiled Macro Facility

Making Macros Available to Your Session

Four basic methods for making macros accessible to your SAS session or job:

- Place all macro definitions in the program before calling them.

- Use a **%INCLUDE** statement to bring macro definitions into the program from external files.

- Use the autocall facility to search predefined source libraries for macro definitions.

- Use the **Stored Compiled Macro Facility** to access permanent SAS catalogs that contain compiled macros.

Advantages to using stored compiled macros:

- The SAS System does not have to submit a macro definition when a macro call is made.

- Nonpermanently stored macros and the autocall facility are also available in the same session.

Note: The Stored Compiled Macro Facility is available starting with Release 6.07 of the SAS System for MVS, CMS, and VMS.

The MSTORED and SASMSTORE= Options

The MSTORED system option controls whether the Stored Compiled Macro
Facility is available:

OPTIONS <u>MSTORED</u>; *STORE MACRO*

OPTIONS NOMSTORED;

The NOMSTORED system option is the default.

The SASMSTORE= system option controls where the macro facility looks for
stored compiled macros:

OPTIONS SASMSTORE = *libref*;

libref   points to an allocated SAS data library. By default, no SAS data
                  library is accessed. (WORK should not be used as a value of
                  libref.)

Note: The MSTORED and SASMSTORE= system options can be set at SAS
       System invocation or with an OPTIONS statement during program
       execution.

       See the previous section for the syntax of specifying invocation options on
       various hosts.

Creating a Stored Compiled Macro

To create a permanently stored compiled macro,

1. submit a LIBNAME statement to point *libref* to the SAS data library where the compiled macro is to be stored (you must have write access)

2. set system options MSTORED and SASMSTORE = *libref*

3. submit the macro definition using the STORE option in the %MACRO statement.

Example: Store the WORDS macro in compiled form in a SAS data library.

```
libname perm 'edc.macro.sasdata' disp=old;
options mstored sasmstore=perm;

%macro words(text,root=w,delim=%str( )) / store
   des='Create Macro Vars from a String';

   %********************************************;
   %* TEXT   is a string to be split into words   ;
   %* ROOT   is base name of the macro variables to  ;
   %*        hold each word (length of ROOT <=5 )    ;
   %* DELIM  is the character(s) used as word breaks ;
   %*                                            ;
   %* Usage: %words(a/b,root=var,delim=/)        ;
   %*              creates global variables       ;
   %*              VAR1=a  VAR2=b  VARSUM=2        ;
   %********************************************;
   %local i word;
   %let i=1;
   %let word=%scan(&text,&i,&delim);
   %do %while(&word ne );
      %global &root&i;
      %let &root&i=&word;
      %let i=%eval(&i+1);
      %let word=%scan(&text,&i,&delim);
   %end;
   %global &root.sum;
   %let &root.sum=%eval(&i-1);
%mend;
```

You can also specify the DES = option to designate an optional 40 character description that will appear in the catalog directory.

Creating a Stored Compiled Macro

If the SASMACR catalog does not exist in the PERM library, it is automatically created.

You can list the contents of the PERM.SASMACR catalog to verify the creation of the compiled macro.

```
proc catalog cat=perm.sasmacr;
    contents;
    title 'Stored Compiled Macro';
quit;
```

```
                    Stored Compiled Macro

            Contents of Catalog PERM.SASMACR

      # Name       Type      Date      Description

      1 WORDS      MACRO     09/29/92  Create Macro Vars from a String
```

Creating a Stored Compiled Macro

Restrictions on stored compiled macros:

- SASMACR is the only catalog in which compiled macros can be stored.

- You should not rename this catalog or its entries.

- You cannot copy compiled macros across operating systems. (You must copy the source program and re-create the stored compiled macro.)

Caution: You should retain the original source program for the macro. The source cannot be re-created from the compiled macro.

For convenience, you can store the source program in an autocall library.

Accessing Stored Compiled Macros

To access stored compiled macros, you must

1. submit a LIBNAME statement to point *libref* to the SAS data library containing a SASMACR catalog (you do not need write access)

2. set system options MSTORED and SASMSTORE = *libref*

3. call any macro stored in *libref*.SASMACR.

Example: Call the WORDS macro in another SAS session.

```
#1    libname perm 'edc.macro.sasdata' disp=shr;
#2    options mstored sasmstore=perm;

#3    %words(this is a test)
             w1   w2 w3 w4

      %put wsum=&wsum;
      %put w1=&w1;
      %put w2=&w2;
      %put w3=&w3;
      %put w4=&w4;
```

Text Written to the SAS Log

```
wsum=4
w1=this
w2=is
w3=a
w4=test
```

Accessing Stored Compiled Macros

You can create multiple SAS data libraries with each data library containing a
SASMACR catalog.

By changing the setting of the SASMSTORE = system option during program
execution, you can control which SASMACR catalog is searched when a macro is
called.

```
options mstored;
libname perm1 'edc.macro.sasdata1' disp=shr;
libname perm2 'edc.macro.sasdata2' disp=shr;
libname perm3 'edc.macro.sasdata3' disp=shr;

options sasmstore=perm2;
%x

options sasmstore=perm1;
%y

options sasmstore=perm3;
%y
```

Accessing Stored Compiled Macros

When a macro call is made (for example, `%mymac`), the macro processor searches for the macro as follows:

1.   as entry MYMAC.MACRO in the WORK.SASMACR catalog

2.   as entry MYMAC.MACRO in the *libref*.SASMACR catalog (providing the MSTORED and SASMSTORE= system options are in effect)

3.   as a file named MYMAC containing the definition for MYMAC (providing the MAUTOSOURCE and SASAUTO= system options are in effect).

The Stored Compiled Macro Facility can be used in conjunction with the autocall facility.

6.3 Memory Management (Optional)

System Options That Control Memory Usage

Two system options control the maximum amount of memory available for storage of macro variables.

MVARSIZE=*n*
> specifies the maximum number of bytes for any macro variable stored in memory ($0 < = n < = 32768$).

MSYMTABMAX=*n*
> specifies the maximum amount of memory available to all symbol tables (global and local combined). The current amount of memory used by symbol tables is found by summing the lengths of all existing macro variable values (excluding automatic variables). The value of *n* can be expressed as an integer or MAX (the largest integer your operating system can represent, typically 2147483647).

These system options can be specified

- at SAS invocation

- during execution with an OPTIONS statement or the OPTIONS window.

Note: The default setting of these system options is host dependent.

System Options That Control Memory Usage

If your program creates a macro variable with a value that

- exceeds the MVARSIZE value, or

- when added to current amount of memory used by user-defined macro variables, exceeds the MSYMTABMAX value,

the macro processor creates a catalog entry in the WORK library to store the macro variable.

Example: Demonstrate storage of macro variables that exceed the MVARSIZE value.

```
%macro sym;
   %global global1 global2 global3 global4;
   %let global1=12345678901;
   %let global3=123456789;
   %let global4=1234567890;

   %local local1 local2 local3;
   %let local1=12345678;
   %let local2=1234567890;
   %let local3=12345678901;
%mend;

options mvarsize=9;
%sym
```

System Options That Control Memory Usage

```
title 'Disk Storage of Macro Variables';
proc catalog cat=work.sasst0;
   contents;
   title2 'Global Variables Exceeding MVARSIZE Value';
run;
```

```
                  Disk Storage of Macro Variables
             Global Variables Exceeding MVARSIZE Value

                  Contents of Catalog WORK.SASST0


      # Name        Type       Date        Description


      1 GLOBAL1     MSYMTAB    04/02/92
      2 GLOBAL4     MSYMTAB    04/02/92
```

```
proc catalog cat=work.sasst1;
   contents;
   title2 'Local Variables Exceeding MVARSIZE Value';
run;
```

```
                  Disk Storage of Macro Variables
              Local Variables Exceeding MVARSIZE Value

                  Contents of Catalog WORK.SASST1


      # Name        Type       Date        Description


      1 LOCAL2      MSYMTAB    04/02/92
      2 LOCAL3      MSYMTAB    04/02/92
```

System Options That Control Memory Usage

Example: Demonstrate storage of macro variables that exceed the
MSYMTABMAX value.

```
%macro sym;
    %global global1 global2 global3 global4 global5 global6;
    %let global1=1234567;
    %let global2=12345678;
    %let global4=1234567890;
    %let global5=123;

    %local local1 local2 local3;
    %let local1=1;
    %let local2=1;
    %let local3=1;

    %let global6=1;
%mend;
options msymtabmax=20;
%sym
%let global7=1;
```

System Options That Control Memory Usage

```
title 'Disk Storage of Macro Variables';
proc catalog cat=work.sasst0;
   contents;
   title2 'Global Variables Exceeding MSYMTABMAX Value';
run;
```

```
                     Disk Storage of Macro Variables
                Global Variables Exceeding MSYMTABMAX Value


                    Contents of Catalog WORK.SASST0

         # Name       Type        Date        Description

         1 GLOBAL4    MSYMTAB     09/29/92
         2 GLOBAL6    MSYMTAB     09/29/92
```

```
proc catalog cat=work.sasst1;
   contents;
   title2 'Local Variables Exceeding MSYMTABMAX Value';
run;
```

```
                     Disk Storage of Macro Variables
                 Local Variables Exceeding MSYMTABMAX Value

                    Contents of Catalog WORK.SASST1

         # Name       Type        Date        Description

         1 LOCAL3     MSYMTAB     09/29/92
```

System Options That Control Memory Usage

Notes on the MVARSIZE and MSYMTABMAX = system options:

- The total amount of memory available to a SAS application program is divided between memory allocated for program execution and that set aside for storage of macro variables.

- When an application program requires a large amount of memory for macro variable storage, these options control the point at which variable storage goes to disk. The reason for this is to prevent macro variable storage from using memory that may be needed for program execution.

- The default values for these options are host dependent.

- If these options are set too high (on some operating systems) and the limits are reached by the application program, excessive memory paging (thrashing) may occur because too little memory remains for program execution.

- If these options are set too low and the limits are reached frequently by the application program, extensive disk I/O may occur as macro variables are created and resolved. This results in decreased performance because of disk I/O.

- The SAS System creates the WORK.SASST0 for global table overflow. WORK.SASST1 is used for the first local symbol table. WORK.SASST*n* is used for other local tables created by nested macro calls.

- Memory for a local table is released when the macro finishes execution. This memory can then be used by other symbol tables. Any catalog entries created are not deleted, they simply are not used any more.

- If a macro variable overflows to disk and is later reassigned a shorter value that can fit in available memory, it is made memory resident. The catalog entry is no longer used, but it is not removed.

When to Change the Defaults

Recommendations:

- Once an application is developed, submit one or more PROC CATALOG steps to see if any WORK.SASST*n* catalogs were created. (Make these the last steps of the program.)

- If none of these catalogs were created, your program did not exceed the system defaults and no further tuning is necessary.

- If the variables that appear in any of these catalogs are used often in the program, you may want to increase the value of one or both of the MSYMTABMAX= or MVARSIZE= system options. Experiment with the values until few, if any, variables are written to disk. If you increase the values significantly, watch for increased CPU usage that can occur if memory thrashing is taking place. In this situation, it may be more efficient to allow macro variables to overflow to disk, depending on the relative costs of CPU time and disk I/O.

When to Change the Defaults

Currently, there is no simple method of obtaining a list of all currently defined macro variables in a symbol table.

For development or debugging purposes, you can set MSYMTABMAX = 0 and force all user-defined macro variables with a nonnull value to be written to disk. Afterwards, a PROC CATALOG step can document the variables created.

Example: List the macro variables created by the program shown below.

```
%macro stats(dsn,var);
   proc summary data=&dsn maxdec=2 nway;
      var &var;
      output out=stats n=n nmiss=nmiss mean=mean
             std=std sum=sum min=min max=max;
   data _null_;
      set stats;
      array nums{*} _numeric_;
      length name $8;
      do i=1 to dim(nums);
         call vname(nums{i},name);
         call symput(name,left(nums{i}));
      end;
   run;
%mend;

options msymtabmax=0;
%stats(perm.all,fee);
proc catalog cat=work.sasst1;
   contents;
run;
```

When to Change the Defaults

Output from PROC CATALOG

```
                         The SAS System

                   Contents of Catalog WORK.SASST1

        #  Name        Type       Date        Description

         1  _FREQ_     MSYMTAB    09/01/92
         2  _TYPE_     MSYMTAB    09/01/92
         3  DSN        MSYMTAB    09/01/92
         4  MAX        MSYMTAB    09/01/92
         5  MEAN       MSYMTAB    09/01/92
         6  MIN        MSYMTAB    09/01/92
         7  N          MSYMTAB    09/01/92
         8  NMISS      MSYMTAB    09/01/92
         9  STD        MSYMTAB    09/01/92
        10  SUM        MSYMTAB    09/01/92
        11  VAR        MSYMTAB    09/01/92
```

6.4 Efficient Macro Programming (Optional)

General Principles

- When designing a SAS application, you should concentrate on making the basic SAS code that macros generate more efficient.

- Incorporating macro coding into an application does not make the application more efficient per se.

- Do not use macros to submit code or execute macro statements that can run as open code.

- Use the **%INCLUDE** statement to include source code into a program when macro programming statements such as **%IF-%THEN** and **%DO** are not required.

- Specify the NOMACRO invocation option for large SAS programs that do not contain macro or macro variable references, or the SYMPUT/SYMGET DATA step functions. (The **%INCLUDE** statement is still available.)

- Use system options such as SYMBOLGEN, MPRINT, and MLOGIC for development and debugging purposes. Turn these options off when the application is in production mode.

- Use local variables instead of global variables whenever possible.

- To conserve memory, consider resetting macro variables to null if they are no longer going to be referenced.

- Check the value of the MSYMTABMAX= system option. Increase the value of this option if you plan to store many macro variables in a symbol table. It is possible for a symbol table to run out of available memory and overflow to a WORK file.

- Check the value of the MVARSIZE= system option. Increase the value of this option if you plan to store a long string in a macro variable. It is possible for a macro variable to run out of available memory and overflow to a WORK file.

6.5 Chapter Summary

To avoid submitting one or more macro definitions in every SAS job that calls macros, you can store your macros in one or more source libraries and designate them as autocall libraries.

If autocall libraries are specified, the macro processor automatically searches them for a macro definition each time a different macro is called. The definition is submitted and the macro is invoked. Calling a macro that is already compiled does not cause a search of the autocall libraries. A requirement is that the program file containing the macro definition must have the same name as its macro. A call to the macro is not required in the program file.

The MAUTOSOURCE and SASAUTOS = system options, must be set to enable searching of autocall libraries. These system options can be specified at job invocation or during program execution.

Another efficient way to make macros available to a job is to store them in compiled form in a SAS data library. To permanently store a compiled macro, you must set two system options, MSTORED and SASMSTORE = *libref*. Then you must submit one or more macro definitions using the STORE option in the %MACRO statement. The compiled form is stored as a catalog entry in *libref*.SASMACR. The source program is not stored as part of the compiled macro. You should always maintain the original source for the macro definitions in case you need to redefine the macro.

The MSTORED and SASMSTORE = *libref* system options must be set to enable searching for existing stored compiled macros. These system options can be specified at job invocation or during program execution.

Autocall libraries and SAS data libraries that contain stored compiled macros can be shared by many users.

The MVARSIZE = and MSYMTABMAX = system options control how the SAS System manages memory for storage of macro variables and symbol tables. You need to be concerned with these options only if your program creates macro variables with very long values or a large number of macro variables. These options control the point at which macro variables are stored on disk instead of in memory.

Chapter Summary

System options:

    MAUTOSOURCE|NOMAUTOSOURCE
    SASAUTOS=
    MSTORED|NOMSTORED
    SASMSTORE=
    MVARSIZE=
    MSYMTABMAX=

Appendix A:
Macro Windows

Introduction

The macro facility enables you to create a windowing environment for front-ending SAS applications. With macro windows, you can

- position text and fields at any location in a window

- control the color and attributes of text and fields

- issue commands from a command line, with function keys, or with a pull-down menu.

Example: Create and display a window to prompt for one field value.

A %WINDOW statement defines the appearance of the window.

```
%window reports
   #1 @20 'Computer Educators Inc.' color=cyan
   #4 @20 'Enter report type:' color=yellow
      +1 type 1 attr=underline required=yes color=yellow /
      @39 'S' color=yellow 'chedule' color=green /
      @39 'C' color=yellow 'ourses' color=green
  #10 @20 'Press ENTER after entering your choice.';
```

A %DISPLAY statement presents the window.

```
%display reports;
```

```
+REPORTS----------------------------------------------------------------+
| Command ===>                                                          |
|                                                                       |
|                     Computer Educators Inc.                           |
|                                                                       |
|                                                                       |
|                     Enter report type: _                              |
|                                         Schedule                      |
|                                         Courses                       |
|                                                                       |
|                                                                       |
|                     Press ENTER after entering your choice.           |
|                                                                       |
+-----------------------------------------------------------------------+
```

Display A.1   REPORTS Window

The %WINDOW Statement

The **%WINDOW** statement

- can be used inside or outside a macro definition

- gives specifications for creating a window

- creates a utility file in the WORK library that is available throughout a SAS session.

General form of the %WINDOW statement:

> **%WINDOW** *window-name options*
> *text | field-specs*
> GROUP = *name*
> *text | field-specs*;

window-name   controls the text that appears in the upper-left corner of the displayed window and the name referenced in a **%DISPLAY** statement. This name must follow SAS naming conventions and is required.

options   specifies optional window characteristics such as color, size, and location.

text | field-specs
   defines text strings or fields to be displayed in the window.

GROUP = *name*
   names a group of text and fields to displayed together. A window can have many groups. Groups can be displayed at different times.

The %WINDOW Statement

Macro windows can be displayed on monochrome or color terminals. If the user's device supports color, you can incorporate color into an application using the values CYAN, YELLOW, WHITE, BLUE, GREEN, PINK, and RED in the COLOR= (C=) option. Many devices support additional colors.

If the user's device supports extended highlighting attributes, you can incorporate them into an application using the values HIGHLIGHT, REV_VIDEO, BLINK, and UNDERLINE in the ATTR= (A=) option.

Selected window options:

COLOR=*color*   specifies the background color of the window (not all devices support this option). The default is BLACK.

COLUMNS=*n*   specifies the number of columns in the window.

ROWS=*n*   specifies the number of rows in the window.

ICOLUMN=*n*   indicates the initial column at which the window is displayed. The default is column 1.

IROW=*n*   indicates the initial row at which the window is displayed. The default is row 1.

KEYS=*libref.catalog.entry*.KEYS
    specifies a catalog with a KEYS entry that defines the key definitions for the window.

MENU=*libref.catalog.entry*.PMENU
    specifies a catalog with a PMENU entry you created with PROC PMENU.

The %WINDOW Statement

The %WINDOW statement also contains specifications for

- text strings

- fields (macro variables).

You control placement, color, and attributes of text strings and fields.

General form of a text string or field:

> *pointer-controls* *'text-string'* *options*
>
> *pointer-controls* *macro-variable* *field-length* *options*

pointer-controls	identify the position of the field.
	Row pointer controls:
	#*n* specifies the row on which the text (field) is located.
	/ moves the pointer to column 1 of the next line.
	Column pointer controls:
	@*n* specifies the column in which text (field) begins.
	+*n* moves the pointer *n* columns to the right.
macro-variable	names a macro variable that a field represents.
field-length	defines the number of columns on the current line available for displaying a variable or inputting a value into a variable.
'text-string'	is the text to display (exactly as entered).

The %WINDOW Statement

Selected text and field options:

ATTR = *attribute*   defines the highlighting attribute for text (field).

COLOR = *color*   defines the color for text (field). The default is WHITE.

Selected field options:

PROTECT = NO|YES
> YES means that no value can be entered in the field. The default is
> NO. (A field can receive a value from an existing macro variable.)

REQUIRED = NO|YES
> YES means the window cannot be closed unless the user provides a
> value for the field. The default is NO.

AUTOSKIP = YES|NO
> NO means the cursor does not jump to the next field when all
> characters of the field are filled. The default is YES.

Example: Define an input field for the macro variable TYPE with a field length
of 8 beginning in row 4 and column 5.

```
%window reports
#4 a5 type 8;
```

Add a text strings field followed by an input field for the variable
DSNAME.

```
%window reports
    #4   a5 'Enter the report type:'
         +1 type 8 c=green required=yes attr=underline
    #10  a5 'Enter data set        :'
         +1 dsname 17 attr=underline;
```

By default, fields are presented in the same color as the window background. To
make fields conspicuous, use the COLOR = or ATTR = option to distinguish the
fields from the background.

The %DISPLAY Statement

The **%**DISPLAY statement

- can be used inside or outside a macro definition.

- creates a windowing environment that is independent of display manager (you can display macro windows with or without the display manager being active).

- opens a window previously defined with a **%**WINDOW statement.

- creates macro variables for fields (same name) if the macro variables do not exist. Standard rules determine whether the variables are created in the global or local symbol table.

- initializes fields with values of corresponding macro variables.

- enables the user to enter text into nonprotected fields.

- executes until the user performs some action to close the window.

- updates macro variables with field values as the window closes.

General form of the **%**DISPLAY statement:

   %DISPLAY *window-name options*;

window-name   can be either *window-name* or *window-name.groupname*.

Selected options:

BELL   produces a beep when a window is displayed.
BLANK   clears the display of any accumulated groups.
NOINPUT   protects all fields in a window from modification.

If there are no required fields, the window is closed when the user

- presses ENTER, or

- issues the END or CANCEL command.

The REPORTS Macro

Example: Write a simple macro that uses **%WINDOW** and **%DISPLAY**
statements to prompt for information and conditionally submit SAS
code.

```
%macro reports;
    %* Define window;
    %window reports
        #1 a20 'Computer Educators Inc.' color=cyan
        #4 a20 'Enter report type:' color=yellow
            +1 type 1 attr=underline required=yes color=yellow /
            a39 'S' color=yellow 'chedule' color=green /
            a39 'C' color=yellow 'ourses' color=green
        #10 a20 'Press ENTER after entering your choice.';

    %* Display window to user;
    %local type;
    %display reports;

    %* Process user responses;
    options nodate nonumber;
    %if %upcase(&type)=S %then %do;
        proc print data=perm.schedule;
            id crsnum;
            title "Course Schedule as of &sysdate";
        run;
        %end;
    %else %if %upcase(&type)=C %then %do;
        proc print data=perm.courses;
            id course;
            title "Courses Offered as of &sysdate";
        run;
        %end;
%mend reports;
```

The REPORTS Macro

The following macro call executes the **%DISPLAY** statement:

    %reports

The user types a c and presses ENTER.

```
+REPORTS----------------------------------------------------------------+
| Command ===>                                                          |
|                                                                       |
|                       Computer Educators Inc.                         |
|                                                                       |
|                       Enter report type: c                           |
|                                         Schedule                      |
|                                         Courses                       |
|                                                                       |
|                                                                       |
|                       Press ENTER after entering your choice.         |
|                                                                       |
+-----------------------------------------------------------------------+
```

Display A.2   REPORTS Window

If the REPORTS macro is called from display manager, program output is automatically displayed in the OUTPUT window.

```
+OUTPUT------------------------------------------------PROC PRINT suspended-+
| Command ===>                                                            |
| NOTE: Procedure PRINT created 1 page(s) of output.                      |
|                    Courses Offered as of 31MAR92                         |
|                                                                         |
|          COURSE     TITLE                        DAYS       FEE          |
|                                                                         |
|          C001       Basic Telecommunications      3       $795          |
|          C002       Structured Query Language      4       $1150         |
|          C003       Local Area Networks            3       $650          |
|          C004       Database Design                2       $375          |
|          C005       Artificial Intelligence        2       $400          |
|          C006       Computer Aided Design          5       $1600         |
|                                                                         |
|                                                                         |
|                                                                         |
|                                                                         |
|                                                                         |
|                                                                         |
+-------------------------------------------------------------R---------+
```

Display A.3   OUTPUT Window

A Complete Application

The following pages show a more sophisticated macro windowing application with the following features:

- A menu window that branches to other windows. Control returns to the menu when other windows close.

- GROUP processing within a window.

- Use of protected fields to display existing information.

- Custom command-line processing.

- Thorough field validation that also copes with any text the user might enter.

- Custom error messages that appear when a field value is invalid.

- Coding that forces the user to exit the application through a menu selection.

- Modular coding for easy maintenance.

The application consists of two macros:

WINDOWS   is a setup macro that contains three **%WINDOW** definitions.

PROCESS   is the main macro that controls window display, interaction with the user, and SAS code generation based on user input.

Outline of the WINDOWS macro:

```
%macro windows;
   %window menu   ... ;
   %window register ... ;
   %window student ... ;
%mend;
```

A Complete Application

Coding for the MENU window:

```
%* Main menu window;
%window menu
  group=start
  #1   @68 sysdate 7 protect=yes color=blue
  #2   @68 sysday  9 protect=yes color=blue
  #3   @68 systime 5 protect=yes color=blue
  #5   @26 'Computer Educators Inc.' color=yellow
  #7   @26 '1' +1 'Course Information' color=cyan
  #9   @26 '2' +1 'Current Registration' color=cyan
  #11  @26 '3' +1 'Student Information' color=cyan
  #13  @26 'L' +1 'Leave Menu' color=cyan
  #16  @26 choice 1 attr=underline required=yes autoskip=no
       +1  '<=== Enter your choice here' color=green
  group=wait
  #18  @22 'Your request is being processed.' attr=blink
  #19  @22 'When you are finished viewing output,'
       color=green
  #20  @22 'press END to return to this menu.' color=green;
```

Display Showing Group WAIT Overlaid on Group START

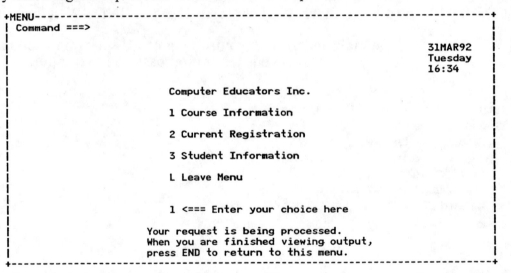

Display A.4   MENU Window

A Complete Application

Coding for the REGISTER window:

```
%* Menu Choice 2 window;
%window register
   group=start
   #1   a68 sysdate 7 protect=yes color=blue
   #2   a68 sysday  9 protect=yes color=blue
   #3   a68 systime 5 protect=yes color=blue
   #5   a26 'Computer Educators Inc.' color=yellow
   #9   a26 'Course Number:' color=cyan +1 crs 2
        attr=underline +1 '(Enter 1-18)'
   #13  a26 'Report: ' color=cyan type 8 attr=underline
        +1 '(Enter LIST or REVENUE)'

        group=wait
   #18 a22 'Your request is being processed.' attr=blink
   #19 a22 'When you are finished viewing output,'
        color=green
   #20 a22 'press END to return to the menu.' color=green;
```

Display Showing Group START Only

```
+REGISTER-------- ---------------------------------------------------+
| Command ===>                                                       |
|                                                                    |
|                                                          31MAR92   |
|                                                          Tuesday   |
|                                                          16:34     |
|                                                                    |
|                      Computer Educators Inc.                       |
|                                                                    |
|                                                                    |
|                                                                    |
|                      Course Number: __ (Enter 1-18)                |
|                                                                    |
|                                                                    |
|                      Report: _____ (Enter LIST or REVENUE)       |
|                                                                    |
|                                                                    |
|                                                                    |
|                                                                    |
|                                                                    |
+--------------------------------------------------------------------+
```

Display A.5   REGISTER Window

A Complete Application

Coding for the STUDENT window:

```
%* Menu Choice 3 window;
%window student
   group=start
   #1   a68 sysdate 7 protect=yes color=blue
   #2   a68 sysday  9 protect=yes color=blue
   #3   a68 systime 5 protect=yes color=blue
   #5   a26 'Computer Educators Inc.' color=yellow
   #9   a16 'Enter portion of last name:' color=cyan
        +1   lastname 12   attr=underline
        +1 '(e.g. Smith)';
```

Display Showing STUDENT Window

```
+STUDENT--------------------------------------------------------+
| Command ===>                                                  |
|                                                               |
|                                                    31MAR92    |
|                                                    Tuesday    |
|                                                    16:34       |
|                                                               |
|                  Computer Educators Inc.                      |
|                                                               |
|                                                               |
|          Enter portion of last name: _____  (e.g. Smith)|
|                                                               |
|                                                               |
|                                                               |
|                                                               |
|                                                               |
|                                                               |
|                                                               |
|                                                               |
|                                                               |
+---------------------------------------------------------------+
```

Display A.6   STUDENT Window

A Complete Application

Notes on the %WINDOW statements:

- The windows are defined separately from the PROCESS macro so that repeated executions of the PROCESS macro do not needlessly redefine existing windows. It is not necessary to submit the WINDOW statements via a macro definition.

- Automatic macro variables are used to initialize protected window fields SYSDATE, SYSDAY, and SYSTIME. The user cannot move to these fields.

- The MENU and REGISTER windows are defined in two groups so that the WAIT group can be merged with the START group after the user has supplied a valid menu choice. See the PROCESS macro for %DISPLAY coding using window groups.

- The options 1,2,3,4,L in the MENU window are selected for simplicity and to allow characters to be entered on the command line to make selections (see the PROCESS macro). If you elect to permit the user to enter values as commands, you must be aware that any text entered on the command line is first interpreted as a SAS global command. If the application uses X as the menu option to exit the application, issuing X on the command line would always take the user out of the window and start a host mode subsession. Also, avoid using any letter or letter combination that might be the beginning of a SAS global command.

- The UNDERLINE attribute is used for all fields, so the user can "see" where the fields are.

- Descriptive text is added to the window to let the user know what the acceptable values are in any field.

A Complete Application

The PROCESS macro:

```
%macro process;
    %local choice cmd crs type lastname;
    %do %until(&choice=L or &cmd=L);
        %let choice=;
        %display menu.start blank;
        %let choice=%qupcase(%superq(choice));
        %let cmd=%qupcase(%superq(syscmd));
        %if &choice=1 or &cmd=1 %then %do;
            %display menu.wait noinput;
            %inc code(schedule);
            %end;
        %else %if &choice=2 or &cmd=2 %then %do;
            %do %until(( &crs ge 1 and &crs le 18) and
                       (&type=LIST or &type=REVENUE));
                %display register.start blank;
                %let type=%qupcase(%superq(type));
                %if &type ne LIST and &type ne REVENUE %then
                    %let sysmsg=Report must be LIST or REVENUE;
                %if &crs lt 1 or &crs gt 18 %then %let sysmsg=
                    Course Number must be between 1 and 18;
            %end;
            %display register.wait noinput;
            %if &type=LIST %then %str(%inc code(reginfo););
            %else %str(%inc code(revenue););
            %end;
        %else %if &choice=3 or &cmd=3 %then %do;
            %let lastname=;
            %display student blank;
            %let lastname=%qupcase(%superq(lastname));
            %if &lastname ne %then %str(%inc code(fsedit););
            %end;
        %else %if &choice=L %then %do; * endsas; %end;
        %else %let sysmsg=Please enter 1, 2, 3 or L;
    %end;
%mend process;
```

A Complete Application

Notes on the PROCESS macro:

- The macro variables named in the **%WINDOW** statement are declared in a **%LOCAL** statement so that subsequent **%DISPLAY** statements do not accidentally update any global variables that may also exist.

- A **%DO %UNTIL** loop is used to control the display of windows. Every time the user releases the MENU window, the current values of the CHOICE and CMD variables are evaluated at the bottom of the loop. The loop terminates only when the user enters L (uppercase or lowercase) in the CHOICE field or on the command line. The CHOICE variable is reset to null before executing the **%DISPLAY** statement so a previous selection does not appear in the window field.

- The initial MENU window shows only the text and fields for the START group (**%display menu.start blank;**).

- The values assigned to the macro variables by the window are quoted and uppercased. This is done to remove the syntactic meaning of any text that may be entered. The **%QUPCASE** function preserves quoting in its argument.

- An optional feature of the application allows menu selections to be entered on the command line. (You can also define a pull-down menu or function keys to issue the menu choices.) To facilitate command processing and error handling, the **%WINDOW** statement creates two automatic macro variables:

  SYSCMD   contains the last command issued in the window (from the command line, function key, or pull-down menu) that was not recognized as a global SAS command. SYSCMD is reset to null at every execution of the **%DISPLAY** statement. You can monitor the value of SYSCMD to create custom commands for an application. You cannot assign values to SYSCMD.

  SYSMSG   contains text to be displayed in the message area (the line below the command line) of the window. You can assign a value to SYSMSG (for example, with a **%LET** statement). The value of SYSMSG is set to null after each execution of a **%DISPLAY** statement.

A Complete Application

Notes on the PROCESS macro (continued):

- If the choice is 1, SAS code is submitted without further prompting. The statement `%display menu.wait noinput;` overlays the WAIT group of MENU window text on top of the currently displayed MENU window and prevents further modification of existing field values. Execution of the %INCLUDE statement causes the display manager OUTPUT window to become active. Once the user views the output and closes the OUTPUT window (END command), control returns to the outer %DO %UNTIL loop. The existing value of CHOICE is reset to null and the MENU window is redisplayed. The BLANK option clears the display of all groups before displaying the START group. Without this option, the WAIT group would still be visible after returning from menu choices 1 or 2.

- If choice 2 is entered, another window is displayed. Note that the values of CRS and TYPE are not reset before the following statement:

      ```
      %display register.start blank;
      ```

  This means that subsequent displays of this window retain the last entered values of CRS and TYPE. You could reset the values to null or to any desired default value.

- If an invalid command or choice is entered, an error message is issued with the SYSMSG variable.

- Processing of the L choice can be handled many ways. In this example, the user returns to the calling environment. By uncommenting the ENDSAS statement, you can terminate the SAS session.

A Complete Application

The SAS code executed by the menu choices:

`%inc code(schedule);` executes this program:

```
* Program for macro menu option 1;

proc print data=perm.all n noobs uniform width=min;
    where crsnum=&crs;
    var name company;
    by location begin;
    title1 "Course Registration as of &sysday, &sysdate";
    title2 "for Course Number &crs";
    options  nodate number pageno=1;
run;
```

`%inc code(reginfo);` executes this program:

```
* Program for macro menu option 2;

proc sql;
    create view temp as
    select courses.course,location,crsnum,
            title,fee,teacher,begin,days
        from perm.courses, perm.schedule
        where courses.course=schedule.course
        order by course;
proc print data=temp noobs uniform;
    by course title;
    id crsnum;
    title "Courses Offered as of &sysday, &sysdate";
    options nodate number pageno=1;
run;
```

A Complete Application

`%inc code(revenue);` executes this program:

```
* Program for macro menu option 2;

proc tabulate data=perm.all format=dollar10.;
   where crsnum=&crs;
   class location begin;
   var fee;
   table location=' '*begin=' '*fee=' '*sum=' ';
   title1 "Total Revenues as of &sysday, &sysdate";
   title2 "for Course Number &crs";
   options nodate number pageno=1;
run;
```

`%inc code(fsedit);` executes this program:

```
* Program for macro menu option 3;

proc fsedit data=perm.students;
   where upcase(scan(name,1,',')) ? "&lastname";
run;
```

Note: All the SAS code in the included files can be developed and tested
        independently of the PROCESS macro. The menu choices could have
        called other macros. The windows that prompt for specific values could
        have passed these values to macros with parameter lists. These techniques
        simplify development and reduce the complexity of the PROCESS macro.

A Complete Application

Initial MENU Window

```
+MENU------------------------------------------------------------------+
| Command ===>                                                         |
|                                                                      |
|                                                          31MAR92     |
|                                                          Tuesday     |
|                                                          16:34       |
|                                                                      |
|                                                                      |
|                        Computer Educators Inc.                       |
|                                                                      |
|                        1 Course Information                          |
|                                                                      |
|                        2 Current Registration                        |
|                                                                      |
|                        3 Student Information                         |
|                                                                      |
|                        L Leave Menu                                  |
|                                                                      |
|                        _ <=== Enter your choice here                 |
|                                                                      |
|                                                                      |
|                                                                      |
+----------------------------------------------------------------------+
```

Display A.7   MENU Window

The MENU Window after a Valid Choice

```
+MENU------------------------------------------------------------------+
| Command ===>                                                         |
|                                                                      |
|                                                          31MAR92     |
|                                                          Tuesday     |
|                                                          16:34       |
|                                                                      |
|                        Computer Educators Inc.                       |
|                                                                      |
|                        1 Course Information                          |
|                                                                      |
|                        2 Current Registration                        |
|                                                                      |
|                        3 Student Information                         |
|                                                                      |
|                        L Leave Menu                                  |
|                                                                      |
|                        1 <=== Enter your choice here                 |
|                        Your request is being processed.              |
|                        When you are finished viewing output,         |
|                        press END to return to this menu.             |
+----------------------------------------------------------------------+
```

Display A.8   MENU Window

A Complete Application

Error Trapping on MENU Window

```
+MENU---------------------------------------------------------------------+
| Command ===>                                                            |
|                                                                         |
|                                                          31MAR92        |
|                                                          Tuesday        |
|                                                          16:34          |
|                                                                         |
|                        Computer Educators Inc.                          |
|                                                                         |
|                        1 Course Information                             |
|                                                                         |
|                        2 Current Registration                           |
|                                                                         |
|                        3 Student Information                            |
|                                                                         |
|                        L Leave Menu                                     |
|                                                                         |
|                                                                         |
|                        4 <=== Enter your choice here                    |
|                                                                         |
|                                                                         |
|                                                                         |
|                                                                         |
+-------------------------------------------------------------------------+
```

Display A.9   MENU Window with Invalid Selection

```
+MENU---------------------------------------------------------------------+
| Command ===>                                                            |
| Please enter 1, 2, 3 or L                                               |
|                                                          31MAR92        |
|                                                          Tuesday        |
|                                                          16:34          |
|                                                                         |
|                        Computer Educators Inc.                          |
|                                                                         |
|                        1 Course Information                             |
|                                                                         |
|                        2 Current Registration                           |
|                                                                         |
|                        3 Student Information                            |
|                                                                         |
|                        L Leave Menu                                     |
|                                                                         |
|                        _ <=== Enter your choice here                    |
|                                                                         |
|                                                                         |
|                                                                         |
+-------------------------------------------------------------------------+
```

Display A.10   MENU Window with Error Message

A Complete Application

Result of Selecting Option 1

```
+OUTPUT-----------------------------------------------PROC PRINT suspended-+
| Command ===>                                                             |
|                                                                          |
|                    Courses Offered as of Tuesday, 31MAR92             1 |
|                                                                          |
| ---------- Course Code=C001 Description=Basic Telecommunications ---------- |
|                                                                          |
|    CRSNUM      LOCATION      FEE        TEACHER        BEGIN    DAYS     |
|                                                                          |
|       1        Dallas       $795    Hallis, Dr. George  04FEB91    3     |
|      13        Boston       $795    Hallis, Dr. George  09SEP91    3     |
|       7        Seattle      $795    Hallis, Dr. George  10JUN91    3     |
|                                                                          |
|                                                                          |
| ---------- Course Code=C002 Description=Structured Query Language ---------- |
|                                                                          |
|    CRSNUM      LOCATION      FEE        TEACHER        BEGIN    DAYS     |
|                                                                          |
|       2        Dallas      $1150   Wickam, Dr. Alice   04MAR91    4     |
|       8        Seattle     $1150   Wickam, Dr. Alice   17JUN91    4     |
|      14        Boston      $1150   Wickam, Dr. Alice   16SEP91    4     |
|                                                                          |
|                                                                          |
+----------------------------------------------------------------R---------+
```

Display A.11   OUTPUT Window

Result of Selecting Option 2

```
+REGISTER------------------------------------------------------------------+
| Command ===>                                                             |
|                                                                          |
|                                                            31MAR92       |
|                                                            Tuesday       |
|                                                            16:34         |
|                                                                          |
|                      Computer Educators Inc.                             |
|                                                                          |
|                                                                          |
|                      Course Number: __ (Enter 1-18)                      |
|                                                                          |
|                                                                          |
|                      Report: _____  (Enter LIST or REVENUE)           |
|                                                                          |
|                                                                          |
|                                                                          |
|                                                                          |
|                                                                          |
|                                                                          |
+--------------------------------------------------------------------------+
```

Display A.12   REGISTER Window

A Complete Application

Error Trapping on REGISTER Window

```
+REGISTER----------------------------------------------------------------+
| Command ===>                                                            |
| Course Number must be between 1 and 18                                  |
|                                                              31MAR92    |
|                                                              Tuesday    |
|                                                              16:34      |
|                                                                         |
|                         Computer Educators Inc.                         |
|                                                                         |
|                                                                         |
|                                                                         |
|                         Course Number: 20 (Enter 1-18)                  |
|                                                                         |
|                                                                         |
|                                                                         |
|                         Report: _____ (Enter LIST or REVENUE)        |
|                                                                         |
|                                                                         |
|                                                                         |
|                                                                         |
|                                                                         |
+-------------------------------------------------------------------------+
```

Display A.13   REGISTER Window with Invalid Course Number

```
+REGISTER----------------------------------------------------------------+
| Command ===>                                                            |
| Report must be LIST or REVENUE                                          |
|                                                              31MAR92    |
|                                                              Tuesday    |
|                                                              16:34      |
|                                                                         |
|                         Computer Educators Inc.                         |
|                                                                         |
|                                                                         |
|                         Course Number: 2  (Enter 1-18)                  |
|                                                                         |
|                                                                         |
|                         Report: LOST     (Enter LIST or REVENUE)        |
|                                                                         |
|                                                                         |
|                                                                         |
|                                                                         |
+-------------------------------------------------------------------------+
```

Display A.14   REGISTER Window with Invalid Report Type

A Complete Application

Result of Selecting Course Number 2 and LIST

```
+OUTPUT-----------------------------------------------PROC PRINT suspended-+
| Command ===>                                                             |
|                                                                          |
|              Course Registration as of Tuesday, 31MAR92          1       |
|                         for Course Number 2                              |
|                                                                          |
| --------------------- Location=Dallas Begin=04MAR91 --------------------- |
|                                                                          |
|         NAME                          COMPANY                            |
|                                                                          |
|         Amigo, Mr. Bill               Assoc. of Realtors                 |
|         Benincasa, Ms. Elizabeth      Hospital Nurses Association        |
|         Brown, Mr. Michael            Swain Diagnostics Inc.             |
|         Divjak, Ms. Theresa           US Weather Services                |
|         Edwards, Ms. Kathy            Allied Wood Corporation            |
|         Gandy, Dr. David              Paralegal Assoc.                   |
|         Hamilton, Ms. Alicia          Security Trust Corp.               |
|         Harrell, Mr. Ken              Information Mart                   |
|         Hill, Mr. Paul                Log Chemical                       |
|         Holbrook, Ms. Amy             Wooster Chemical                   |
|         James, Ms. Anne               San Juan Gas and Electric          |
|         Kelly, Ms. Tamara             Cetadyne Technologies              |
|         Kling, Mr. Kelly              NBA Insurance Co.                   |
+---------------------------------------------------------------R---------+
```

Display A.15   OUTPUT Window

A Complete Application

Result of Selecting Option 3

```
+STUDENT------------------------------------------------------------+
| Command ===>                                                       |
|                                                                    |
|                                                          31MAR92   |
|                                                          Tuesday   |
|                                                          16:34     |
|                                                                    |
|                       Computer Educators Inc.                      |
|                                                                    |
|                                                                    |
|          Enter portion of last name: _____  (e.g. Smith)      |
|                                                                    |
|                                                                    |
|                                                                    |
|                                                                    |
|                                                                    |
|                                                                    |
|                                                                    |
|                                                                    |
+--------------------------------------------------------------------+
```

Display A.16   STUDENT Window

```
+STUDENT------------------------------------------------------------+
| Command ===>                                                       |
|                                                                    |
|                                                          31MAR92   |
|                                                          Tuesday   |
|                                                          16:34     |
|                                                                    |
|                       Computer Educators Inc.                      |
|                                                                    |
|                                                                    |
|          Enter portion of last name: ed        (e.g. Smith)        |
|                                                                    |
|                                                                    |
|                                                                    |
|                                                                    |
|                                                                    |
|                                                                    |
|                                                                    |
|                                                                    |
+--------------------------------------------------------------------+
```

Display A.17   STUDENT Window with Field Value Supplied

A Complete Application

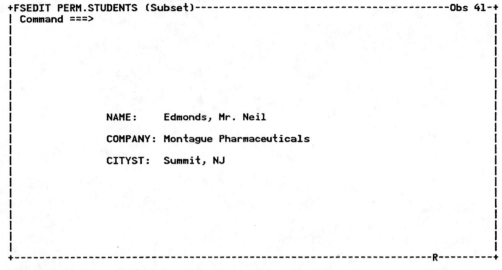

```
+FSEDIT PERM.STUDENTS (Subset)-------------------------------------------Obs 41-+
| Command ===>                                                                  |
|                                                                               |
|                                                                               |
|                                                                               |
|                                                                               |
|                                                                               |
|            NAME:    Edmonds, Mr. Neil                                         |
|                                                                               |
|            COMPANY: Montague Pharmaceuticals                                  |
|                                                                               |
|            CITYST:  Summit, NJ                                               |
|                                                                               |
|                                                                               |
|                                                                               |
|                                                                               |
|                                                                               |
|                                                                               |
+----------------------------------------------------------------R---------+
```

Display A.18   FSEDIT Window with a Subset of Observations

In summary, macro windows

- can be used for front-ending applications when SAS/AF software is not available.

- can submit tailored batch programs or SAS code for any SAS product.

- are harder to design and debug than SAS/AF applications, especially multiple window applications.

- pose field validation problems when you want to validate items such as data set names, variable names, existing variable values. (See Appendix B for information on how to approach this. Examples in Chapter 5 also show how to do more advanced field validation.)

- do not require display manager, but you must find a substitute for the OUTPUT window if you want to show output to the user. PROC PRINTTO along with PROC FSLIST can be used for this purpose.

- can be activated with a noninteractive program submission or an autoexec file. (You cannot display windows from batch jobs.)

Appendix B:
Dictionary Tables

Utility Windows

The SAS System internally maintains detailed information about

- external files defined to the current session

- SAS data libraries defined to the current session

- all SAS data sets and catalogs

- current settings of system options.

Interactively, you can use utility windows to display some of this information:

FILENAME   displays currently active filerefs and corresponding host filenames.

LIBNAME   displays currently active librefs and corresponding engines and host path names.

DIR   displays SAS filenames, their member type (DATA, VIEW, CATALOG and so on), and whether indexes are defined for DATA members.

VAR   displays variable name, length, format informat, key (index), and label information for member types DATA and VIEW.

CATALOG   displays name, type, description, and date last updated for entries.

OPTIONS   display current settings of system options.

Utility Windows

Selected utility windows are shown below.

```
+LIBNAME--------------------------------------------------------------------+
| Command ===>                                                              |
|                                                                           |
|      Libref     Engine      Host Path Name                                |
|                                                                           |
|      PERM       V606        EDU.MACRO.SASDATA                             |
|  _   SASHELP    V607        SDC.SAS6CURR.SASHELP                          |
|  _   SASUSER    V607        EDC.TEMP.SASUSER                              |
|  _   WORK       V607        SYS92094.T103614.RA000.EDC.R0000089           |
|  _                                                                        |
|                                                                           |
+---------------------------------------------------------------------------+
```

Display B.19   LIBNAME Window

```
+DIR------------------------------------------------------------------------+
| Command ===>                                                              |
|                                                                           |
| Libref: PERM                                                              |
| Type: ALL                                                                 |
|                                                                           |
|      SAS File  Memtype    Indexed                                         |
|                                                                           |
|  _   ALL       VIEW                                                       |
|  _   COURSES   DATA                                                       |
|  _   REGISTER  DATA                                                       |
|  _   SCHEDULE  DATA                                                       |
|  _   STUDENTS  DATA                                                       |
|                                                                           |
+---------------------------------------------------------------------------+
```

Display B.20   DIR Window

```
+VAR------------------------------------------------------------------------+
| Command ===>                                                              |
|                                                                           |
| Libref: PERM                                                              |
| Dataset: COURSES                                                          |
|                                                                           |
|      Variable Length Format         Informat        Key Label            |
|                                                                           |
|  _   COURSE   $4                                     N   Course Code      |
|  _   TITLE    $25                                    N   Description      |
|  _   DAYS     8     1.              1.               N   Course Length    |
|  _   FEE      8     DOLLAR5.        DOLLAR5.         N   Course Fee       |
|                                                                           |
+---------------------------------------------------------------------------+
```

Display B.21   VAR Window

Note: All utility windows can be accessed during foreground SAS executions
whether or not display manager is active.

Dictionary Tables

You can also access this information during program execution (interactive, noninteractive, or batch) through *dictionary tables.*

Dictionary tables

- are special read-only utility tables created by PROC SQL

- are dynamically maintained during program execution

- are accessed via the special DICTIONARY libref

- have reserved table and column names

- have rows containing all the information displayed in SAS utility windows (and more)

- can be read directly by PROC SQL only.

The DESCRIBE statement in PROC SQL prints the column definitions and shows the nature of the data contained in these tables.

```
proc sql;
    describe table dictionary.extfiles;
```

Output of the DESCRIBE Statement Written to the SAS Log

```
NOTE: SQL table DICTIONARY.EXTFILES was created like:

create table DICTIONARY.EXTFILES
  (
   FILEREF char(8) label='Fileref',
   XPATH char(80) label='Path Name',
   XENGINE char(8) label='Engine Name'
  );
```

The following pages show output in the SAS log from DESCRIBE statements on all other dictionary tables.

Dictionary Tables

Partial SAS Log

```
NOTE: SQL table DICTIONARY.MEMBERS was created like:

create table DICTIONARY.MEMBERS
  (
   LIBNAME char(8) label='Library Name',
   MEMNAME char(8) label='Member Name',
   MEMTYPE char(8) label='Member Type',
   ENGINE char(8) label='Engine Name',
   INDEX char(8) label='Indexes',
   PATH char(80) label='Path Name'
  );
```

Dictionary Tables

Partial SAS Log

```
NOTE: SQL table DICTIONARY.TABLES was created like:

create table DICTIONARY.TABLES
  (
   LIBNAME char(8) label='Library Name',
   MEMNAME char(8) label='Member Name',
   MEMTYPE char(8) label='Member Type',
   MEMLABEL char(40) label='Dataset Label',
   TYPEMEM char(8) label='Dataset Type',
   CRDATE num format=DATETIME informat=DATETIME label='Date Created',
   MODATE num format=DATETIME informat=DATETIME label='Date Modified',
   NOBS num label='Number of Observations',
   OBSLEN num label='Observation Length',
   NVAR num label='Number of Variables',
   PROTECT char(3) label='Type of Password Protection',
   COMPRESS char(8) label='Compression Routine',
   REUSE char(3) label='Reuse Space',
   BUFSIZE num label='Bufsize',
   DELOBS num label='Number of Deleted Observations',
   INDXTYPE char(9) label='Type of Indexes'
  );
```

Partial SAS Log

```
NOTE: SQL table DICTIONARY.VIEWS was created like:

create table DICTIONARY.VIEWS
  (
   LIBNAME char(8) label='Library Name',
   MEMNAME char(8) label='Member Name',
   MEMTYPE char(8) label='Member Type',
   ENGINE char(8) label='Engine Name'
  );
```

Dictionary Tables

Partial SAS Log

```
NOTE: SQL table DICTIONARY.COLUMNS was created like:

create table DICTIONARY.COLUMNS
  (
   LIBNAME char(8) label='Library Name',
   MEMNAME char(8) label='Member Name',
   MEMTYPE char(8) label='Member Type',
   NAME char(8) label='Column Name',
   TYPE char(4) label='Column Type',
   LENGTH num label='Column Length',
   NPOS num label='Column Position',
   VARNUM num label='Column Number in Table',
   LABEL char(40) label='Column Label',
   FORMAT char(16) label='Column Format',
   INFORMAT char(16) label='Column Informat',
   IDXUSAGE char(9) label='Column Index Type'
  );
```

Dictionary Tables

Partial SAS Log

```
NOTE: SQL table DICTIONARY.INDEXES was created like:

create table DICTIONARY.INDEXES
  (
   LIBNAME char(8) label='Library Name',
   MEMNAME char(8) label='Member Name',
   MEMTYPE char(8) label='Member Type',
   NAME char(8) label='Column Name',
   IDXUSAGE char(9) label='Column Index Type',
   INDXNAME char(8) label='Index Name',
   INDXPOS num label='Position of Column in Concatenated Key',
   NOMISS char(3) label='Nomiss Option',
   UNIQUE char(3) label='Unique Option'
  );
```

Partial SAS Log

```
NOTE: SQL table DICTIONARY.CATALOGS was created like:

create table DICTIONARY.CATALOGS
                        The SAS System

  (
   LIBNAME char(8) label='Library Name',
   MEMNAME char(8) label='Member Name',
   MEMTYPE char(8) label='Member Type',
   OBJNAME char(8) label='Object Name',
   OBJTYPE char(8) label='Object Type',
   OBJDESC char(40) label='Object Description',
   MODIFIED char(8) label='Date Modified',
   ALIAS char(8) label='Object Alias'
  );
```

Dictionary Tables

Partial SAS Log

```
NOTE: SQL table DICTIONARY.OPTIONS was created like:

create table DICTIONARY.OPTIONS
  (
   OPTNAME char(16) label='Session Option Name',
   SETTING char(200) label='Session Option Setting',
   OPTDESC char(80) label='Option Description'
  );
```

You can write PROC SQL programs to extract information from any dictionary
table.

```
title 'Information from DICTIONARY.TABLES';
proc sql;
    select memname,nvar,nobs,modate
        from dictionary.tables
        where libname='PERM';
```

Information from DICTIONARY.TABLES

Member Name	Number of Variables	Number of Observations	Date Modified
COURSES	4	6	15NOV91:08:33:43
REGISTER	3	434	15NOV91:08:33:43
SCHEDULE	5	18	15NOV91:08:33:43
STUDENTS	3	207	06MAR92:12:40:53

SASHELP Views

To simplify access by other components of the SAS language, the SAS System provides VIEW files that any SAS program can read. These views are stored in the SASHELP data library.

```
+DIR----------------------------------------------------------------+
| Command ===>                                                       |
|                                                                    |
| Libref: SASHELP                                                    |
| Type: VIEW                                                         |
|                                                                    |
|      SAS File  Memtype    Indexed                                  |
|                                                                    |
|   _  VCATALG   VIEW                                                |
|   _  VCOLUMN   VIEW                                                |
|   _  VEXTFL    VIEW                                                |
|   _  VINDEX    VIEW                                                |
|   _  VMEMBER   VIEW                                                |
|   _  VOPTION   VIEW                                                |
|   _  VSACCES   VIEW                                                |
|   _  VSCATLG   VIEW                                                |
|   _  VSLIB     VIEW                                                |
|   _  VSTABLE   VIEW                                                |
|   _  VSTABVW   VIEW                                                |
|   _  VSVIEW    VIEW                                                |
|   _  VTABLE    VIEW                                                |
|   _  VVIEW     VIEW                                                |
|                                                                    |
+--------------------------------------------------------------------+
```

Display B.22   DIR Window Showing VIEW Files Stored in SASHELP

The following view files extract all the information stored in corresponding dictionary tables.

```
proc sql;
   describe view sashelp.vextfl;
```

Output of DESCRIBE Statement Written to the SAS Log

```
NOTE: SQL view SASHELP.VEXTFL is defined as:

      select *
        from DICTIONARY.EXTFILES;
```

The following pages show output in the SAS log from the DESCRIBE statement on other views.

SASHELP Views

Partial SAS Log

```
NOTE: SQL view SASHELP.VMEMBER is defined as:

      select *
        from DICTIONARY.MEMBERS;
```

```
NOTE: SQL view SASHELP.VTABLE is defined as:

      select *
        from DICTIONARY.TABLES;
```

```
NOTE: SQL view SASHELP.VVIEW is defined as:

      select *
        from DICTIONARY.VIEWS;
```

```
NOTE: SQL view SASHELP.VCOLUMN is defined as:

      select *
        from DICTIONARY.COLUMNS;
```

SASHELP Views

Partial SAS Log

```
NOTE: SQL view SASHELP.VINDEX is defined as:

      select *
        from DICTIONARY.INDEXES;
```

```
NOTE: SQL view SASHELP.VCATALG is defined as:

      select *
        from DICTIONARY.CATALOGS;
```

```
NOTE: SQL view SASHELP.VOPTION is defined as:

      select *
        from DICTIONARY.OPTIONS;
```

SASHELP Views

The following messages in the SAS log show some of the information stored in
DICTIONARY.MEMBERS that is extracted by the view files.

```
NOTE: SQL view SASHELP.VSLIB is defined as:

        select distinct LIBNAME, PATH
            from DICTIONARY.MEMBERS
        order by LIBNAME asc;
```

```
NOTE: SQL view SASHELP.VSTABLE is defined as:

        select LIBNAME, MEMNAME
            from DICTIONARY.MEMBERS
            where MEMTYPE='DATA'
        order by LIBNAME asc, MEMNAME asc;
```

```
NOTE: SQL view SASHELP.VSVIEW is defined as:

        select LIBNAME, MEMNAME
            from DICTIONARY.MEMBERS
            where MEMTYPE='VIEW'
        order by LIBNAME asc, MEMNAME asc;
```

SASHELP Views

The following messages in the SAS log show some of the information stored in DICTIONARY.MEMBERS that is extracted by the view files.

```
NOTE: SQL view SASHELP.VSTABVW is defined as:

      select LIBNAME, MEMNAME, MEMTYPE
        from DICTIONARY.MEMBERS
        where (MEMTYPE='VIEW') or (MEMTYPE='DATA')
      order by LIBNAME asc, MEMNAME asc;
```

```
NOTE: SQL view SASHELP.VSCATLG is defined as:

      select LIBNAME, MEMNAME
        from DICTIONARY.MEMBERS
        where MEMTYPE='CATALOG'
      order by LIBNAME asc, MEMNAME asc;
```

```
NOTE: SQL view SASHELP.VSACCES is defined as:

      select LIBNAME, MEMNAME
        from DICTIONARY.MEMBERS
        where MEMTYPE='ACCESS'
      order by LIBNAME asc, MEMNAME asc;
```

Note: These SASHELP views were created for your convenience. You can create your own views of dictionary tables with PROC SQL.

SASHELP Views

Views created with PROC SQL can be read with the DATA step or any SAS procedure.

```
title 'Information from SASHELP.VTABLE';
proc print data=sashelp.vtable noobs label;
   var memname nvar nobs modate;
   where libname='PERM';
run;
```

Information from SASHELP.VTABLE

Member Name	Number of Variables	Number of Observations	Date Modified
COURSES	4	6	15NOV91:08:33:43
REGISTER	3	434	15NOV91:08:33:43
SCHEDULE	5	18	15NOV91:08:33:43
STUDENTS	3	207	06MAR92:12:40:53

Applications Using Dictionary Tables

The information contained in the dictionary tables has a wide variety of applications in macro-based systems:

You can write programs that

- verify the existence of SAS files or external files before you attempt to access them

- verify the existence of variables before you attempt to process them

- monitor variable attributes such as type, length, format, and informat

- check the number of observations (both total and deleted) in a SAS data set before processing it

- perform dynamic SAS data library maintenance based on when SAS files or catalog entries were created or last updated

- control how certain files can be processed (for example, view files created by SQL (engine = SASESQL) cannot be updated)

- verify the existence of indexes before submitting WHERE clauses

- detect whether data sets are in a compressed form

- monitor the level of password protection that is assigned to a SAS data set.

Applications Using Dictionary Tables

Example: Write a macro that verifies the existence of a SAS data set.

```
%macro chkdsn(lib,dsn);
    %global sqlobs;
    %let lib=%upcase(&lib);
    %let dsn=%upcase(&dsn);
    proc sql noprint;
        select * from dictionary.members
            where libname="&lib" and memname="&dsn";
    quit;
    %if &sqlobs=0 %then
        %put NOTE: &lib..&dsn is not defined.;
%mend;
```

The automatic macro variable SQLOBS contains the number of rows generated by a SELECT statement.

This program illustrates how you could use the CHKDSN macro.

```
%macro printds(libref,member);
    %chkdsn(&libref,&member)
    %if &sqlobs %then %do;
        proc print data=&libref..&member;
        title "LISTING OF %upcase(&libref).%upcase(&member)";
        run;
        %end;
%mend;
```

If you use macro windows to prompt for names of data sets or variables, you should perform some form of error checking to prevent submitting code that will not execute.

Applications Using Dictionary Tables

The results of various calls to the PRINTDS macro are shown below.

```
%printds(perm,courses)
```

```
                    LISTING OF PERM.COURSES

   OBS     COURSE     TITLE                     DAYS      FEE

    1      C001       Basic Telecommunications    3      $795
    2      C002       Structured Query Language   4      $1150
    3      C003       Local Area Networks         3      $650
    4      C004       Database Design             2      $375
    5      C005       Artificial Intelligence     2      $400
    6      C006       Computer Aided Design       5      $1600
```

```
%printds(perm,student)
```

Partial SAS Log

```
NOTE: PERM.STUDENT is not defined.
```

```
%printds(per,students)
```

Partial SAS Log

```
NOTE: PER.STUDENTS is not defined.
```

Applications Using Dictionary Tables

Example: Write a macro that creates a macro variable containing a list of all SAS
data sets in a given SAS data library. Use the specified libref as the
name of the macro variable.

```
%macro dsnlist(libref,refresh=N);
   options nosource;
   %let libref=%upcase(&libref);
   %global &libref;
   %if &&&libref= or &refresh ne N %then %do;
      data _null_;
         set sashelp.vstabvw;
         where libname="&libref";
         call symput('dsn',trim(memname));
         call execute('%let &libref=&&&libref &dsn;');
      run;
      %let &libref=%str( &&&libref );
      %end;
   options source;
%mend dsnlist;


%dsnlist(PERM)
%put Library PERM contains data sets:;
%put &perm;
```

Text Written to the SAS Log

```
Library PERM contains data sets:
 ALL COURSES REGISTER SCHEDULE STUDENTS
```

Applications Using Dictionary Tables

The PRINTDS macro calls the DSNLIST macro to perform error checking.

```
%macro printds(lib,dsn);
   %dsnlist(&lib)
   %let lib=%upcase(&lib);
   %let dsn=%upcase(&dsn);
   %if %index(&&&lib,%str( &dsn ))>0 %then %do;
      proc print data=&lib..&dsn;
         title "Listing of &lib..&dsn";
      run;
      %end;
   %else %do;
      %if &&&lib= %then
         %put ERROR: Libref &lib is not defined.;
      %else %do;
         %put ERROR: &lib..&dsn doesn%str(%')t exist.;
         %put %str(          &lib data sets are:&&&lib);
         %end;
      %end;
%mend printds;
```

The following calls to the PRINTDS macro show the SAS log messages generated.

```
%printds(perm,course)
```

```
ERROR: PERM.COURSE doesn't exist.
       PERM data sets are: ALL COURSES REGISTER SCHEDULE STUDENTS
```

```
%printds(per,courses)
```

```
ERROR: Libref PER is not defined.
```

Applications Using Dictionary Tables

Example: Write a macro that removes observations marked for deletion from a SAS data set only if the data set contains deleted observations.

```
%macro fsedit(dsn);
    %let dsn=%upcase(&dsn);
    proc fsedit data=perm..&dsn;
    run;
    proc sql noprint;
        select delobs into :delobs
            from dictionary.tables
            where libname="PERM" and memname="&dsn";
    quit;
    %put NOTE: &delobs observations were deleted from &dsn;
    %if &delobs>0 %then %do;
        data perm..&dsn;
            set perm..&dsn;
        run;
        %end;
%mend;
%fsedit(students)
```

Text Written to the SAS Log

```
NOTE:        6 observations were deleted from STUDENTS
```

Index

Your Turn

If you have comments about SAS Institute's instructor-based training or the written materials used for this course, please let us know by writing to us with your ideas.

Please write to the Course Development Department, Education Division, SAS Institute Inc., SAS Campus Drive, Cary, NC 27513.